SHINING BRIGHT, SHINING BLACK

WIDE EYED EDITIONS

CONTENTS

WELCOME to THIS BOOK!

The team who brought you *Young, Gifted and Black* and *Young, Gifted and Black, Too* is returning with this lovingly rebound treasury of both books, a celebration of 100 iconic and inspiring Black artists, activists, dreamers, doers, makers, athletes, healers, leaders, thinkers, and inventors. We have a shiny new name—and some exciting new material, including a detailed timeline and a set of thought-provoking discussion questions at the back of the book. But we remain inspired by the song "To be Young, Gifted and Black," which iconic singer Nina Simone wrote as a tribute to her friend Lorraine Hansberry, the first Black woman to write a Broadway play.

Since the song was initially performed in 1969, it has been covered and sampled by many artists who have uniquely made it their own and, in a way, issued an invitation to the next generation to follow in the tradition of taking inspiration and motivation from the heroes who came before them.

More than ever, it needs repeating—our lives matter.

This treasury is a tribute to our ancestors and to the next generation of Black changemakers, but it is also a call to you. It's a chance for you to learn more, to be inspired, and to also ask yourself—and others—questions, start discussions, and be motivated by these remarkable heroes.

The books we read and the media we consume deeply influence our understanding of who we are and what we can be—if you can SEE it, you can BE it. And of course, books also impact how we understand each other. So while much has changed since Lorraine's play and Nina's song were written, the stories in movies, at school, and on television often show a limited view of the achievements and experiences of people of color. That's why we're highlighting the talent and contributions of Black changemakers from around the world— for readers of all backgrounds to discover.

Join us, then, on a journey through time, across borders, and even through space for a small but mighty snapshot of the infinite number of celebrated and unsung heroes worldwide, including yourselves and the people you care about.

We both believe in the power of creating what we need to see. Although our icons from past and present illustrate countless different ways to live, work, love, and light up the world, they were and are in many ways just like you; singular, unique, incomparable, and themselves. Thank you for being perfectly and irreplaceably you.

You are one of our heroes, too.

Jamia Wilson & Andrea Pippins

JAMIA WILSON

ANDREA PIPPINS

HOW THIS BOOK WORKS

In this book, 100 icons from around the world showcase Black achievement from the 1500s to present day. Ordered chronologically from their birthdate, each entry includes an illustrated snapshot, along with a short biography of the rich lives of these incredible figures.

This treasury also features bonus material at the back of the book, including a **detailed timeline** showcasing their achievements in the larger context of world events. A helpful **glossary** follows and includes many of the occupations mentioned within these pages.

While each of the 100 visionary leaders, pioneers, and helpers we've highlighted have unique strengths and have endured various heartbreaks and triumphs, they all share in a fearless pursuit of their dreams and goals. We hope that you're just as encouraged by the artists, activists, doers, makers, healers, and dreamers who bravely paved the way for us to have a brighter future. And with this in mind, we've added a **"Trailblazer" section**, detailing a sample of the "firsts" accomplished by these remarkable heroes.

As you read through the pages of this book, we hope you feel moved to investigate and discover more. The treasury's final section contains a set of **discussion questions** to ask yourself or to share with others. It's an opportunity to reflect and to ponder the larger questions and ideas. You may find yourself strongly affected by some of the personal histories you read about, and you can ask yourself:

What do these heroes inspire you to make or do with your own gifts?

As you turn each page, meet familiar faces, and learn about new remarkable heroes from around the world, these discussion questions can help you discover some of your own dreams, achievements, challenges, experiences, and curiosities. So:

How do you plan to write your name on the present and future pages of history?

We all deserve to see ourselves represented positively in stories, and we hope this book makes you feel celebrated, hopeful, connected, seen, and part of a global community, wherever you are.

Let's look to the lessons of the past while imagining what's possible when we dare to be bold.

Juan's remarkable mastery of Latin earned him the name "Juan Latino."

JUAN LATINO
(C. 1518–C. 1594)

Poet, professor, and self-described "teacher of the young," Juan de Sessa was the first Afro-Spaniard to publish a book in Latin verse in 1573.

Juan was born around 1518 and was enslaved to a noble Spanish family for much of his life. As a child, Juan had a thirst for knowledge. He accompanied his enslaver's son Gonzalo to school, carrying Gonzalo's books and sitting in on classes. Juan's intelligence was noticed, and he was soon allowed to take part. He impressed his teachers with his brilliance and talent for Latin, Greek, and writing poetry.

After school, Juan went on to study at the University of Granada, earning a Bachelor of Arts degree in 1546. Juan then fell in love with and married a Spanish noblewoman. Their union was one of Spain's first legally recognized mixed-race partnerships.

Juan's achievements didn't stop there. He became a lecturer at the University of Granada and spent 20 years teaching students grammar and Latin. Juan also wrote and published three volumes of Latin poetry, including his epic poem, *Austrias Carmen*. He is remembered for his rich, boundary-breaking life.

QUEEN NANNY
(C. 1686-C. 1733)

Queen Nanny led the Maroons, a community of formerly enslaved Africans in Jamaica, in a fight for freedom from slavery and British colonial rule. Notorious for her rebellion and use of clever guerilla tactics, Nanny saw her enemies defeated time and time again.

In Nanny's time, many African people were forcibly transported to colonies in the Americas, where they were forced to work on plantations. Nanny was part of a group who had escaped enslavement and formed settlements high in the Blue Mountains of Jamaica. Nanny united her community and fought to stay free. She organized raids on plantations and battles against British troops. Her warriors knew the land, and would lay in wait, striking their enemies with precision. It's thought that Nanny's leadership and strategies helped free hundreds of enslaved people. Tired of losing, the British eventually negotiated with the Maroons, agreeing to their demands for free settlements.

Queen Nanny's role in the Maroons' resistance has been remembered and passed down in oral history for centuries. She is known as *"The Mother of All Jamaicans,"* and remains an enduring symbol of resistance.

JAMAICA

Nanny's portrait appears on the Jamaican $500 bill.

TOUSSAINT L'OUVERTURE

Celebrated as "the Father of Haiti," Toussaint L'Ouverture was a notorious leader in the fight for freedom from slavery and colonial rule. His legendary leadership paved the way for Haiti's establishment as the first free state founded by enslaved people.

Toussaint was born into slavery on the Breda plantation in Saint-Domingue (known today as Haiti), a French colony on the western section of the Caribbean Island of Hispaniola. Toussaint and other enslaved people lived there in captivity under white minority rule.

Toussaint was a talented person. He learned to read and write and, in addition to Haitian Creole and the African tribal language he spoke, he learned French and Latin. He was given extra responsibilities on the Breda plantation farm and was known for his skills training horses and working with medicinal plants. In his early thirties, Toussaint gained his freedom and got married.

For almost 20 years, he raised his children with his wife Suzanne and worked as a paid steward and coachman on the plantation. In 1791, there was a slave revolt and Toussaint felt convinced to join the struggle. He proved his worth as a soldier and leader, training, organizing, and recruiting formerly enslaved people. He famously declared: *"Unite yourselves to us, brothers, and fight with us for the same cause."*

First, he allied with the Spanish who controlled the other side of Hispaniola. Then, in 1794 when the French abolished slavery, he switched sides and fought the Spanish, seizing control of the whole of Hispaniola. Though Saint-Domingue was still a French colony, Toussaint was leading it, and in 1801 he declared a new constitution (a set of principles and laws) for the island that made him governor-general for the rest of his life.

The French grew wary of his power. In 1802, they arrested Toussaint and sent him to prison, where he died in 1803. A year later, resistance forces resumed the fight, and won, declaring Saint Domingue an independent nation named Haiti.

Famous for finding openings in his enemies' defences, Toussaint adopted the surname "L'Ouverture," meaning "the opening" in French.

ALEXANDER PUSHKIN

(1799-1837)

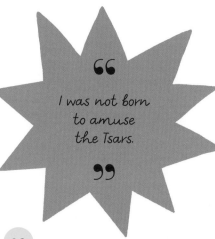

> " I was not born to amuse the Tsars. "

Alexander Pushkin was a poet, novelist, and playwright. He remains one of Russia's most famous writers, with many of his works translated around the world.

Alexander was the great-grandson of a military leader and governor named Gannibal, who had been kidnapped as a child from Cameroon, Africa. Gannibal's enslavers gave him to the Tsar of Russia, Peter the Great, who then freed and adopted him.

Born into the Tsar's inner circle, Alexander studied multiple languages, especially French. As a child, he enjoyed reading, meeting with his parents' visitors, and talking with local workers for hours on end. One of his nurses, Arina, shared folktales that later inspired his poems and his famous novel *Eugene Onegin*.

After his schooling, Alexander began to write about a fairer world for workers. His poem "Ode to Liberty" was a favorite among rebels who fought for social change. This angered Tsar Alexander I, who exiled Alexander to a distant part of Russia in punishment.

Despite this, Alexander persisted in writing until his death and is remembered as one of the greatest literary figures in history.

ALEXANDRE DUMAS
(1802-1870)
VILLERS-COTTERÊTS, FRANCE

Alexandre Dumas is the famed author of *The Count of Monte Cristo* and *The Three Musketeers*. His work has been translated into more than 100 languages.

Known for his historical adventure novels, French author and playwright Alexandre was born Dumas Davy de la Pailleterie in 1802.

During his childhood, he lived in Viller-Cotterêts with his mother, Marie Louise and father, Thomas-

Alexandre. His father was the highest ranking black man in a European army at that time. Aged 20, he moved to the city of Paris to scribe for King Louis Phillippe. There, he occupied himself with Romantic drama and comedic storytelling. Due to the popularity of his writing, Dumas was able to build his prized castle, the Château de Monte-Cristo.

Sadly, his fortune transformed into debt in 1851, which forced him into exile. At the end of his life, the writer who famously coined "*All for one, and one for all*" had published over 100,000 pages of work.

MARY SEACOLE

(1805-1881)

KINGSTON, JAMAICA

Heroine of the Crimean War, Mary Seacole, pioneered as a nurse who cared for British soldiers at the battlefront.

As a child, young Mary learned about Caribbean medicine from her mother, a free black Jamaican woman. A natural healer, she practiced her nursing skills dolls and pets before caring for humans.

By 1854, Mary was living in London when the suffering of soldiers in the Crimean War went public. At the start of the war, her application to join Florence Nightingale's nursing team was rejected—like many others who were refused due to their race or class. Determined to help, Mary put her nursing skills to use and went to war at her own expense.

In 1855, she built the British Hotel near Balaklava to care for injured soldiers. She helped contain the cholera outbreak by distributing remedies in hospitals on the Crimean frontlines.

Although she passed away in 1881, *"Mother Seacole"* is remembered for bravely running a business, kindly caring for ill and injured warriors, and defying discrimination during an era when black women's rights were limited.

HARRIET TUBMAN

(1822–1913)

DORCHESTER COUNTY, MARYLAND · USA

Nicknamed Moses, Harriet Tubman led hundreds of enslaved people to freedom as one of the most notorious conductors on the Underground Railroad.

Harriet Tubman was born into slavery in Maryland. She worked as a house servant from age five onwards. Aged 12, she was forced to labor in the fields. Then, she was struck by an overseer for defending another enslaved person, sustaining a head injury that resulted in lifelong visions and vivid dreams.

In 1849, Harriet ran away in fear of being sold. By following the North Star, she traveled to Philadelphia. Her escape inspired her to rescue her family and many others. She made the risky trip south at least 13 times, using the Underground Railroad, a network of safe houses and allies.

Harriet, who was also an advocate for women's rights, said she *"Never lost a single passenger"* when she spoke about the many enslaved people she escorted to freedom.

YAA ASANTEWAA (1840-1921)

Yaa Asantewaa was a warrior queen in the Asante Empire (part of present-day southern Ghana) who led a fierce resistance against the British invasion and occupation of her people's lands.

Born to farmer parents, Yaa Asantewaa was the eldest of two children. Her name follows a tradition of naming children after the day they were born: girls born on a Thursday ("Yawoda" in Akan) are often named "Yaa."

As she came of age, Yaa studied cultural traditions, developed a skill for farming, sang in family and sacred rituals, sculpted clay objects, and worshipped at her family shrine. Later, she became a mother to Nana Ama Serwaah of Boankra, her only child.

Her community was part of the Asante Empire, a powerful kingdom with rich traditions, and her brother was a chief within the empire. He gave Yaa the role of Queen Mother. Part of this role was to protect the "Golden Stool"—the royal throne and great symbol of power.

Yaa took her role seriously and when the British mined the land for gold, deported Asante leaders, taxed the people, and demanded they hand over the Golden Stool, she rebelled. When the male leaders were unsure what to do, Yaa, a champion of women, notoriously declared: "*. . . if you, the men of Asante, will not go forward, then we will. We the women will. I shall call upon my fellow women . . .*"

After rallying the chiefs and recruiting troops, Yaa was made a war leader and her army besieged the British battalion in 1900. For months, they battled the British forces.

Despite her valiant rebellion, Yaa was eventually captured by the British and exiled to the Seychelles for the rest of her life. Although Yaa didn't live to see independence and the formation of Ghana in 1957, her legacy of leadership, dedication, and courage are commemorated through museums, schools, and awards established in her name and memory. She remains a symbol of independence and resilience today.

GHANA (ASANTE EMPIRE)

The rebellion became known as the "War of the Golden Stool" or "Yaa Asantewaa War."

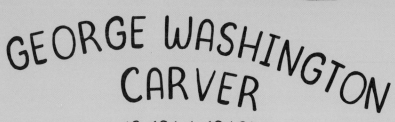

GEORGE WASHINGTON CARVER
(C. 1964-1943)

DIAMOND, MISSOURI · USA

Known as "the plant doctor," scientist George Washington Carver devised over 100 products using peanuts as his only crop.

George Washington Carver was born into slavery in Diamond Grove, Missouri during the Civil War. At one week old, he was kidnapped by outlaws. He eventually returned to his birthplace toward the end of the war.

George was a sickly child, so he focused on household chores and gardening. When slavery was abolished, he learned to read and write from the family that formerly enslaved him.

After being rejected from college due to discrimination, he studied art, piano, and botany in Iowa. He went on to become the first black student and teacher at Iowa State College.

George's success led him to direct the department of agriculture at the Tuskegee Institute. His findings and inventions helped poor cotton farmers adapt their crops and improve their health. *Time* magazine called him *"Black Leonardo,"* in reference to the Italian artist and inventor Leonardo da Vinci, for his ground-breaking agricultural artistry.

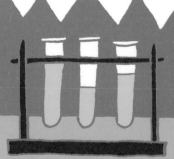

NANJEMOY, MARYLAND·USA

MATTHEW HENSON

(1866-1955)

Matthew Alexander Henson was the first African-American Arctic explorer. Over the course of 18 years, he joined many exciting and challenging expeditions in search of the North Pole.

Born to poor tenant farmers who passed away during his childhood, Matthew became a dishwasher at Janey's Home-Cooked Meals Café to support himself when he was about eleven years old. One of his favorite parts of the work was learning about the customers' lives. He was especially fascinated by sailors and any interesting voyages.

Aged 12, he walked forty miles from his home to Baltimore to work on a merchant boat. Once he was hired, he learned how to read and write from the ship's captain. Always adventurous, Matthew sailed all around the world.

In 1890, he joined voyager Robert Peary's first Arctic expedition across the northern tip of Greenland. He went on to cover almost 10,000 miles on dogsleds across Greenland and Canada.

Matthew's team made history by becoming the first explorers to reach the North Pole in 1909. Matthew declared, *"I think I'm the first man to sit on top of the world."*

MADAM C.J. WALKER

(1867-1919)

(SARAH BREEDLOVE) DELTA, LOUISIANA·USA

Madam C.J. Walker was the first black female millionaire. She invented a line of best-selling African-American hair products.

Madam C.J. Walker was born Sarah Breedlove on the plantation where her parents had been enslaved during the Civil War. After losing both her parents at seven years old, she moved to Mississippi with her sister, Louvenia, to build a better future.

In 1906, Sarah married C.J. Walker and took his name. When a common scalp condition led to hair loss, she developed a homemade treatment that she began selling to other black women with the same ailment.

Walker went on to build a beauty empire. She placed adverts with photos of her own "before and after" shots in African-American newspapers, sold her products in churches, and trained others to share stories about the Madam C.J. Walker lifestyle.

Known for saying "*I got my start by giving myself a start,*" Walker paved the way for others to live their dreams. She created jobs for women and supported educational scholarships and charities. She also traveled to the White House to urge President Wilson to end racial violence.

Activist W.E.B. Du Bois co-founded the National Association for the Advancement of Colored People.

William grew up in Great Barrington, a community with few black residents in Massachusetts. His father left the family when William was a child.

Aged 16, his mother passed away, leaving William out in the world on his own. In the face of hardship, William became the first black student to graduate from his high school. He said *"Education and work are the levers to uplift a people."*

In 1885, William went to study at Fisk University in Tennessee. He enjoyed having more access to black culture at Fisk, but his experiences with discrimination led him to examine the roots of racism. His studies inspired him to become an activist.

William, now known as "W.E.B.," went on to become one of the leading black voices of the 20th century, and cofounded the National Association for the Advancement of Colored People, a multiracial civil rights group that still advances justice today.

W.E.B. DU BOIS
(1868–1963)
GREAT BARRINGTON, MASSACHUSETTS
USA

U.S.A.

Some of the brothers' best-known projects include the Martin Luther King, Jr. Memorial in Washington, D.C., The National Civil Rights Museum in Memphis, Tennessee, and The Carnegie Library at Fisk University, in Nashville, Tennessee.

MOSES AND CALVIN MCKISSACK

(1879-1952 & 1890-1968)

Moses McKissack III and his brother Calvin McKissack established the first Black-owned professional architectural firm in the United States.

The seeds of the McKissack brothers' passion for building are rooted in their family history. Their grandfather, Moses McKissack I, was a Black enslaved brickmaker in Tennessee, who later gained his freedom. He had 14 children with his Cherokee Indigenous wife, Mirian. Their son, Gabriel Moses McKissack II, made his career in construction, becoming famous for his expert carpentry skills. Gabriel passed his knowledge to his sons, Moses III and Calvin.

Moses and Calvin were educated in segregated schools in Pulaski, Tennessee. By the late 1800s, Moses was working as an architect's apprentice. His reputation bloomed and soon he was building houses in Alabama and Tennessee. In 1905, Moses relocated to Nashville.

Younger brother Calvin attended Fisk University in Nashville, then worked as an architect in Texas before moving back to Nashville, too. Calvin worked with his brother, but also held different university and high school teaching jobs.

In 1921, the state of Tennessee required all architects to be licensed and registered. Both Moses and Calvin completed a correspondence course in architecture from the prestigious Massachusetts Institute of Technology and became the first African Americans to take the licensing exam in 1922. The licensing authorities believed the brothers would fail because of their race, but Moses and Calvin succeeded.

They teamed-up full time and McKissack and McKissack became one of Tennessee's first registered architectural firms. Their commissions included Pearl High School, the Morris Memorial Building, and Tennessee State University's Memorial Library. Then, in 1942, the firm was hired by the US government to design and build Tuskegee Army Airfield in Alabama. At the time, the $5.7 million contract was the biggest federal contract ever awarded to a Black-owned company.

Moses and Calvin went on to become licensed in more than 20 states. Moses's son William and his wife Leatrice later took on the business, and the brothers' legacy lives on through their descendants, who still build incredible architecture today!

BESSIE COLEMAN

PILOT LICENSE

(1892-1926)

ATLANTA, TEXAS · USA

Bessie Coleman was an airshow PILOT, and the first African American and Indigenous American to stage a public flight.

One of 13 kids, Bessie trekked for four hours a day to her one-room school in Texas. Always a high flyer, she excelled at mathematics and reading. When she wasn't studying, she helped out on her family farm and attended church. Her determination and drive led to her gaining a place at Langston University in Oklahoma. But college fees were expensive, and Bessie had to leave after completing only one semester.

Aged 23, Bessie heard stories from World War I pilots during her job as a manicurist. Their adventures inspired her. Since US flight schools denied women and Black people entry, Bessie became a licensed pilot in France. Although a crash ended the aviator's dream of opening a school for Black fliers, her legacy continues. Mae Jemison, the first Black female astronaut in space, brought a photo of *Brave Bessie* on her first mission.

Ann Lowe was the go-to designer for many American leaders, stars, and trendsetters of her time. Known for her artistry, she became the first internationally known African American fashion designer.

The great-granddaughter of an enslaved Black woman and a white enslaver, Ann was born into a family of seamstresses in Clayton, Alabama. Ann's mother died when she was 16, leaving her with sewing orders to finish for important clients. Ann rose to the challenge, soon earning a name for herself.

Word of Ann's talent spread, leading her to travel to Florida to work as a dressmaker for a wealthy client. Later, she moved to New York City, where she enrolled at the S.T. Taylor Design School. Here, Ann was segregated from white students. Though her work was often used as a model of excellence in class, she often faced discrimination.

After graduating, Ann established her dress salon, designing for the rich and famous and high-end stores. She designed and created future First Lady Jacqueline Bouvier Kennedy's iconic wedding gown.

At the time, she was given little credit, but today her designs are showcased in museums such as the Metropolitan Museum of Art and the National Museum of African American History and Culture.

ANN LOWE

(1898–1981)

U.S.A.

" All the pleasure I have had, I owe to my sewing. "

Chief, teacher, and activist, Albert Luthuli made history for being the first African awarded the Nobel Peace Prize in 1960. He led millions of people in a nonviolent campaign to end apartheid in South Africa.

Albert was born in Solusi Mission Station in present-day Zimbabwe. When he was 10 years old, he and his mother moved to South Africa, where his parents were originally from. There, Albert learned the traditions of his Zulu community. After school, Albert worked as a teacher and, in 1936, he was elected as a chief of the Zulu community in Groutville, KwaZulu-Natal.

He was involved in many causes and worked to improve the lives of his fellow citizens. In 1945, he joined the African National Congress (ANC)—a political party that sought to unite African people and defend their rights. In 1948, the South African government introduced the system of apartheid. Albert became president of the ANC and campaigned against the system, leading protests and strikes.

To try to stop him, authorities arrested and accused him of treason. But Albert refused to stop and his dedication to nonviolent resistance earned him the Nobel Peace Prize. He spent the rest of his life campaigning and inspiring others.

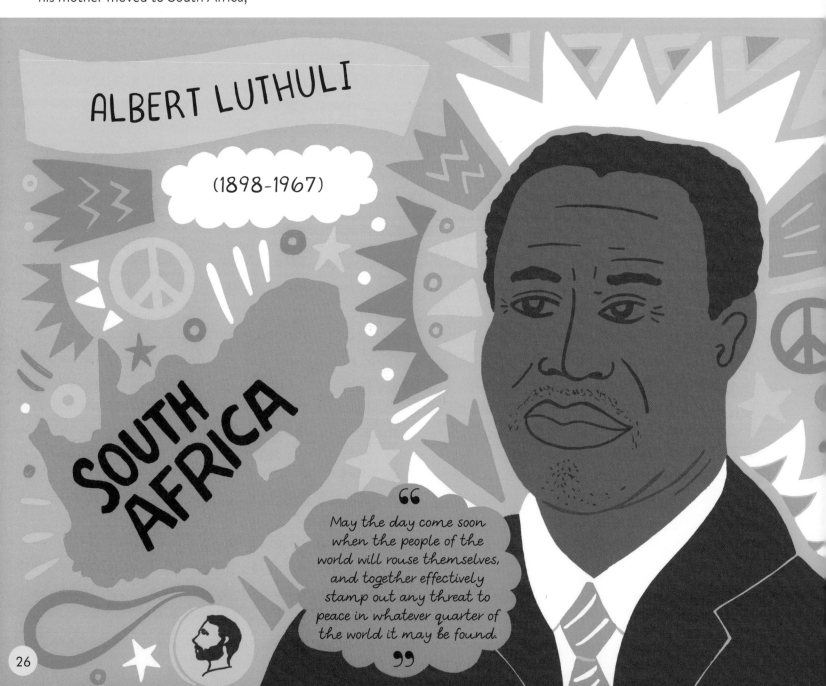

ALBERT LUTHULI

(1898-1967)

SOUTH AFRICA

"
May the day come soon when the people of the world will rouse themselves, and together effectively stamp out any threat to peace in whatever quarter of the world it may be found.
"

LOUIS ARMSTRONG

(1901-1971)

NEW ORLEANS, LOUISIANA USA

Known as "Satchmo" or "Pops," Louis Armstrong is one of history's most influential entertainers. "Satch" is best known for his songs "What a Wonderful World" and "La Vie En Rose."

Louis was born in a section of New Orleans that was so rough it was dubbed "The Battlefield." After his father left, he was forced to drop out of school so he could collect junk and deliver coal to help support his family.

As a youth, Louis was arrested when he shot his stepfather's gun in the air during a party. The police confined him to a boys' home as a punishment. There,

he learned to play the cornet and discovered his passion for music.

In 1914, horn player Joe "King" Oliver taught Louis and let him play in his place. This earned him a gig with the finest band in town, Kid Ory's. Louis rose to fame in the 1920s for his vocal and trumpet mastery.

Although he started as a jazz performer, he was hailed as a virtuoso for his rare talent and stage presence. His swinging sounds and acting helped the Grammy Hall of Fame winning singer capture the hearts of his generation and beyond.

LANGSTON HUGHES
(1901-1967)
JOPLIN, MISSOURI · USA

Langston Hughes is one of the most well-known WRITERS of the Harlem Renaissance—an artistic movement that took place after World War One.

Langston was raised by his grandmother in Lawrence, Kansas. When she passed away, Langston moved to Illinois, and then Ohio to live with his mother. In Illinois, the talented young writer was elected class poet by his schoolmates.

Inspired by writers Carl Sandburg and Walt Whitman, he contributed to his high school's literary magazine and yearbook.

Following graduation, Langston lived in Mexico for a year with his father. During this time, he published "The Negro Speaks of Rivers" in *The Crisis* magazine. The lyrical traveler served as a steward on a ship from Africa to Spain, and later published poetry in Paris.

The man who wrote "*Hold fast to dreams, for if dreams die, life is a broken-winged bird that cannot fly,*" took his own advice and became a prolific writer despite hardship. After releasing his first book of poetry in 1926, he penned over 60 literary works including memoirs, novels, musicals, opera, children's poetry, short stories, and plays.

Surgeon and researcher Charles Richard Drew's pioneering work on the storage of blood plasma saved lives. Charles made history as the first African American to earn a Doctor of Medical Science degree in 1940 and became the first Black surgeon elected to serve on the American Board of Surgery in 1941.

Charles spent his childhood with his parents and siblings in Washington D.C.'s Foggy Bottom. Intelligent and driven, he earned a degree from Amherst College before enrolling in medical school at Canada's McGill University. Charles next attended Columbia University where he discovered a groundbreaking technique for preserving blood. This meant blood could be stored for longer in special "blood banks."

When World War II began, Charles was asked to help supply blood to the United Kingdom where it could save the lives of the wounded. Charles got to work on the "Blood for Britain" campaign, overseeing the preservation and transportation of thousands of blood donations.

In 1941, Charles became the director of the first American Red Cross Blood Bank, but resigned in protest a year later, unable to support the then US government's baseless policy of separating blood donations by race.

Charles's legacy lives on through the countless lives saved using his research.

CHARLES R. DREW

(1904-1950)

"
There is no scientific basis for the separation of the bloods of different races.
"

U.S.A.

JOSEPHINE BAKER

(1906-1975)
ST. LOUIS, MISSOURI • USA

Josephine Baker was an American-born French entertainer, World War II resistance spy, and a civil rights activist.

The daughter of a laundress and a drummer, Josephine grew up in poverty. Forced to work as a servant to provide food for her family, she took on adult responsibilities when she was eight.

By 13, Josephine ran away from home. When she wasn't working, she performed on street corners. Her talent landed her a job dancing, singing, and acting for local vaudeville shows.

Several years later, she made her Broadway debut in the musical "Shuffle Along." Her success propelled her to France in 1925, where she captured the hearts of audiences. Within a decade, Josephine became one of the most well-known stars in Europe after dancing in a banana skirt during her iconic show, "La Folie du Jour." When World War II broke out, she helped support the allies by working as a spy. While she toured Europe, she passed on secret messages that were hidden in her sheet music. After the war, she went on to adopt 12 children.

As the first African American to serve as a Supreme Court justice, lawyer and civil rights leader Thurgood Marshall played a critical role in confronting legal segregation in the United States and advancing equal justice for all.

Thurgood was born in Baltimore, Maryland. As a child, he was a gifted student and leader on the school debate team. Dinnertime discussions with his father helped fuel his passion for logic and law. He was also a little mischievous and, after one incident of mischief at school, he was made to memorize the entire United States Constitution!

He went on to study law at Howard University and graduated at the top of his class. He then began work for the National Association for the Advancement of Colored People (NAACP). He spent over two decades at the NAACP, arguing and winning many cases that fought racism, policies of segregation, and discrimination. His work helped to secure and defend the rights of people of color, earning him the nickname "*Mr. Civil Rights.*"

In 1967, President Lyndon B. Johnson nominated Thurgood for the Supreme Court, the nation's highest court of justice, where he served until he retired in 1991, three years before his death.

THURGOOD MARSHALL

(1908–1993)

U.S.A.

LAW

Thurgood's legal vision was based on doing the right thing. He once said: "You do what you think is right and let the law catch up."

JESSE ★ OWENS

(1913-1980)

OAKVILLE, ALABAMA · USA

Once known as the fastest man in the world, Olympic track and field champion Jesse Owens won four gold medals at the 1936 Berlin Games.

James Cleveland Owens was a frail child whose condition sometimes prevented him from helping his family with farm work. When he was eight, they moved from Alabama to Ohio for better opportunities. When a teacher wrote his initials "J. C." as "Jesse" by mistake, he decided to keep it.

By fifth grade, Jesse grew into a strong runner and joined the track team. After setting records in the 100 and 200-yard dash, and the broad jump, his coach described him as appearing to float in air.

Jesse's success attracted college recruiters. By this time, Jesse was a young father, and so attended Ohio State University (O.S.U.) to stay near family. Jesse reigned as O.S.U.'s first black sports team captain. Nicknamed the "Buckeye Bullet," he set three world records and made history as an Olympic champion.

Civil rights activist Rosa Parks refused to give up her bus seat to a white passenger and ignited the Montgomery Bus Boycott.

A rebel with a cause, Rosa was born to a carpenter and a teacher in Alabama. When she was two, she moved to her grandparents' farm. Her grandparents were formerly enslaved people who lived in Pine Level, a town that separated people based on their skin color.

Growing up, Rosa heard the Ku Klux Klan, a group that promotes hate, pass by her home at night. She feared that her home would be burned down. Despite the risks, Rosa fought back when white children bullied her.

In 1955, Rosa refused to give up her seat in the "colored section" of a city bus to a white person after the "whites only" section was full. When asked if she stayed seated because she was tired, Rosa said, *"The only tired I was, was tired of giving in."*

She was arrested, and black people all over the city stopped using the buses in protest. This forced the city of Montgomery to end segregation on public buses.

Rosa was an activist for the rest of her life and supported many causes. The US Congress named her *"the mother of the freedom movement."* Today, her legacy lives on in all who refuse to obey unfair rules that hurt and divide people.

SISTER ROSETTA THARPE

Legendary singer and guitarist Sister Rosetta Tharpe is called "the original soul sister" and the "Godmother of rock 'n' roll" for her huge influence on music from the 1920s right up to the present day.

Rosetta was born in Cotton Plant, Arkansas, to parents who worked in the cotton fields. Her father Willis was a singer, and her mother Katie played the mandolin while singing and preaching. Little Rosetta started playing the guitar at age four.

In 1921, Rosetta's mother included her as a performer in her gospel troupe, which sang Christian music. Known as "the singing guitar-playing miracle," Rosetta crisscrossed the American South with her mother's church until they settled in Chicago. By the time she moved to New York City in the 1930s, Rosetta was becoming famous not only for her incredible musical abilities but for taking gospel music out of the church and into public places.

By age 23, Rosetta had released her first recorded song, "Rock Me," using the stage name Sister Rosetta Tharpe. Throughout the 1940s, she recorded more hit songs and toured with fellow Black musician Marie Knight until going solo in 1951. One of her songs,

"Down by the Riverside," was chosen by the US Library of Congress' registry, a list of sound recordings deemed important for the entire country to hear.

Rosetta wowed listeners with her energetic vocals, expert electric guitar playing, and an all-new sound that formed the beginnings of rock 'n' roll. Audiences in America and Europe loved her powerful performances and joyful spirit. During a time when women electric guitarists were rare, and Black musicians faced open discrimination, Rosetta paved the way, becoming an inspiration to many people.

Rosetta died in 1973, but her music and her mark are still felt—in 1998 she was featured on a US postage stamp and in 2018 she was inducted into the Rock & Roll Hall of Fame.

66

Can't no man play like me.

99

NELSON MANDELA

(1918-2013)

MVEZO TRANSKEI, SOUTH AFRICA

Nelson Mandela was a Nobel Peace Prize winner and the former PRESIDENT of South Africa.

President Mandela was born on the river banks of a village in South Africa to parents in the Tembu people's royal family. They gave him the name "Rolihlahla," which means "troublemaker" in the Xhosa language, a title that he would live up to for the rest of his life.

Rolihlahla loved learning and said *"Education is the most powerful weapon we can use to change the world."* He went to a mission school where his teacher started calling him "Nelson."

Nelson was treated cruelly due to apartheid, a system that used laws to discriminate against people based on their skin color. Although they were the majority, Black people had no input into how their country was run and were barred access to education and fair wages. They were also met with violence when they stood up for their rights.

Nelson spoke out about human rights, which caused important people to stop trading with South Africa. He was jailed for 27 years, initially in a small cell in Robben Island prison, for standing up for equality.

Getting into "good trouble" helped Nelson transform his country. Although he had "A Long Walk to Freedom," as his memoir is named, he is celebrated for promoting peace and building bridges between people. His later work with former President F.W. de Klerk helped end apartheid and steered South Africa's peaceful transition to majority rule when he became president in 1994. He lived by the words *"It always seems impossible until it's done."*

Nelson passed away in 2013, but his legacy of resistance, hope, and dignity lives on in South Africa's emerging "born-free" generation.

GEORGE WASHINGTON GIBBS JR.

(1916–2000)

Naval Officer George Washington Gibbs Jr. was a pioneer. He became the first African American sailor to reach Antarctica, receiving the silver US Antarctic Expedition Medal.

Born in Jacksonvillle, Florida, George enlisted in the US Navy at just 19. Four years later, he was selected to join an expedition to Antarctica. Due to racist policies in the US Navy at the time, the only position he could hold was "mess attendant." His duties included cooking and cleaning.

George was frustrated by his lack of options and the racism he faced, but the opportunity to set foot on the frozen lands of Antarctica was one he had to take. Throughout the expedition, George rose to every challenge and was praised for his energy and loyalty. After the expedition, George fought in World War II, surviving the torpedoing of his ship and helping others stay alive too. He left the US Navy in 1959 and went on to earn a university degree and have a successful career in business. He became a civil rights organizer and never stopped challenging unfairness and racial discrimination.

U.S.A.

Gibbs Point on the Antarctic Peninsula is named in George's honor.

KATHERINE JOHNSON

(1918-2020)

WHITE SULPHUR SPRINGS
WEST VIRGINIA · USA

Physicist and mathematician Katherine Johnson calculated the flight path for the first American mission to space.

Katherine always loved counting. She liked the certainty of math because *"You're either right or you're wrong."* Starting high school at 10, and college at 15, her appetite for learning helped her blaze through courses.

Despite her dream of becoming a mathematician, she believed her options were limited to "being a nurse or a teacher" due to barriers to equal education and employment. Nonetheless, Katherine focused on geometry, the study of lines, shapes, and angles, throughout her college years.

Her determination paved her way to NASA (National Aeronautics and Space Administration). There, she calculated pathways for spacecrafts to orbit Earth and land on the moon. Her work opened doors for women and African Americans in the fields of mathematics and computing.

In 2015, she received the Presidential Medal of Freedom, the highest civilian award in the USA.

JACKIE ROBINSON
(1919–1972)

Jack "Jackie" Roosevelt Robinson was the first African American to play modern Major League Baseball and become inducted into the Baseball Hall of Fame.

Jackie was born in Cairo, Georgia, but grew up in California. Money was tight and life wasn't easy for his family. Jackie's escape was sports. With his family's encouragement he pursued his passions. In high school and college, he played baseball, tennis, football, basketball, and earned medals in track-and-field events. In 1945, after serving in the US army, Jackie began to play baseball for the Negro National League, but it wasn't long before his talent was noticed in the Major Leagues.

Despite facing death threats and racist heckling, he broke baseball's color barrier (the practice of excluding players of African descent) and joined the Brooklyn Dodgers in 1947, winning Rookie of the Year, gaining countless fans, and helping the Dodgers win time and again.

Jackie also dedicated his voice to civil rights activism, helping establish Black-owned businesses, and speaking alongside Martin Luther King, Jr.

U.S.A.

Jackie's number, #42, was retired from the sport by the Major League in 1997 in honor of his legacy.

SHIRLEY CHISHOLM

(1924-2005)

BROOKLYN, NEW YORK • USA

Shirley Chisholm was the first African-American congresswoman in the United States.

Shirley began her life as the first of four daughters born to immigrant parents. At five, she sailed to Barbados to live on her grandmother's farm, while her parents worked in New York. She went to a one-room schoolhouse with strict teachers who helped her refine her speaking and writing talent.

In 1939, Shirley returned to Brooklyn. At Brooklyn College, a professor noticed her "quick mind and debating skills" and urged her to pursue politics. She joined the debate team and started her own club after another group barred Black people.

Shirley never asked for permission to be included. She took her rightful place and paved the way for others. She said, *"If they don't give you a seat at the table, bring a folding chair."*

Her drive led Shirley to become the first African-American candidate to run for president in 1972. In 2015, President Obama named her a recipient of the Presidential Medal of Freedom.

BERTINA LOPES
(1924-2012)

World-renowned painter and sculptor Bertina Lopes made African-inspired art using bright colors, shapes, and textures. Her work was shaped by her interest and knowledge of African folktalkes and the politics of her time.

The daughter of a Mozambican mother and Portuguese father, Bertina was born in Mozambique, which was occupied and controlled by Portugal at the time. In high school, Bertina moved to Portugal, studying with inspiring and well-known artists.

In 1953, she returned to Mozambique, teaching and painting there. During this time, many Mozambicans wanted independence from Portugal's rule, and Bertina used her art to voice her own anti-colonial and anti-discrimination views. Forced to leave her home due to her politics and associations with other figures of resistance, she relocated to Italy in 1964, where she continued to create her one-of-a-kind art until her death. She has received many awards in recognition for her work.

MOZAMBIQUE

Bertina created art for 70 years of her life. She often used her work to tell stories and express her views.

FRANTZ FANON (1925-1961)

Frantz Omar Fanon was a French West Indian psychiatrist and thinker whose writings explored and criticized racism and colonialism.

A descendent of enslaved Africans, Frantz was born in Martinique in the Caribbean, a French colony at the time. At 18, Frantz moved to France to fight in World War II and later studied medicine and psychiatry there. Throughout his life, Frantz experienced and witnessed racism—colonized people, Black soldiers, and everyday Black citizens were treated unjustly. Frantz wrote many books on the subject, including *Black Skin, White Masks*, and *The Wretched of the Earth*. He later moved to Algeria in Africa, another French colony, and spent his last years fighting for its independence.

Despite his short life (he died at 36), Frantz' legacy is far-reaching. He became a hero in the anti-colonial and anti-racist struggle. His work has inspired many thinkers and activists, and influenced liberation movements in Ghana, the United States, South Africa, and elsewhere.

> 66
> When we revolt it's not for a particular culture. We revolt simply because, for many reasons, we can no longer breathe.
> 99

HANS MASSAQUOI
(1926-2013)

Hans-Jürgen Massaquoi was an author, journalist, US Army paratrooper, and magazine editor. Born in Hamburg, Germany to a white German mother and a Black Liberian-Vai father, Hans was one of a tiny population of Black Germans living in Germany during World War II.

After the war, Hans moved to the United States, fighting in the Korean War as a paratrooper. He later earned a journalism degree, becoming an author and editor for influential magazines that discussed and celebrated African American culture and news.

Hans wrote a memoir about his experience growing up Black in Germany when the Nazis were in power. He urged readers to fight injustice like the cruelty and racism he experienced during his youth.

> 66
> It is never too soon to confront bigotry and racism whenever, wherever, and in whatever form it raises its ugly head.
> 99

Acclaimed filmmaker, actor, and director, Sir Sidney Poitier was the first Bahamian and African-American to win an Academy Award for Best Actor.

Born while his Bahamian parents were vacationing in Florida, Sidney was a preemie. Although he wasn't expected to survive, he grew stronger and moved to his family's tomato farm in the Bahamas.

Sidney's father was worried he would become involved in mischief and sent him to live with his brother in Miami at 14. But at 16, he moved to New York City after encountering the Ku Klux Klan, a violent and racist hate group.

Making a living in the city was difficult. While working odd jobs, he spotted a flyer about acting opportunities at the American Negro Theatre. Since he couldn't sing or dance like black actors were expected to do at the time, he focused on acting.

Sidney stuck to his motto: "*To simply wake up every morning a better person than when I went to bed.*" He went on to become the first African-American to win an Oscar for his performance in *Lilies of the Field*. His acting positively changed portrayals of black people in the media.

SIDNEY POITIER
(1927-2022)
MIAMI, FLORIDA • USA

MAYA ANGELOU

(1928-2014)

ST. LOUIS, MISSOURI·USA

Celebrated for her poetry, essays, screenplays, and acting, Maya Angelou was a writer and civil rights activist.

Before Maya Angelou became a household name, she had a difficult childhood. After her parents separated, Maya and her brother traveled by themselves to live in Stamps, Arkansas, with their grandmother. Once there, her uncle taught her to read, which inspired her passion for books.

At seven, Maya was attacked by her mother's boyfriend. Her distress caused her to stop speaking for years. Later, she based her autobiography, *I Know Why the Caged Bird Sings*, on this experience.

As an adult, Maya became San Francisco's first black female cable car conductor and the first African-American woman to have her screenplay produced.

The author of seven memoirs fought for equal rights for women and African Americans throughout her life. She said, *"You alone are enough. You have nothing to prove to anybody."*

CORETTA SCOTT KING

Correta Scott King was an American civil rights leader who devoted her life to racial equality, gender justice, and world peace.

Coretta was born in rural Alabama and raised on the family farm. The great-granddaughter of a formerly enslaved person, Coretta was the third of four children in a family with African American, Irish, and Indigenous ancestors.

Due to laws that separated people based on their race in the American South, Coretta saw and experienced racial injustice early in life. She attended a segregated school, which she had to walk miles to get to while buses took local white children to a different school. Seeing these injustices made her want to combat racism, and in college she became involved in civil rights activism.

After college, Coretta—a gifted singer—enrolled at the New England Conservatory of Music in Boston, Massachusetts, where she met and fell in love with American civil rights hero Martin Luther King, Jr.

Coretta and Martin married in 1953 and went on to have four children. They shared the same goals and beliefs and campaigned together for change, social justice, and peace, until Martin was killed in 1968.

Only three weeks after her husband's assassination, Coretta addressed a crowd of thousands in New York City with an anti-war speech found in Martin's pocket on the day of his death. Coretta ensured Martin's work, words, and dreams for a better world would not be forgotten, and she successfully campaigned to make Martin Luther King, Jr. Day (January 16th) a national holiday in the United States.

Coretta also continued to champion causes she believed in. She protested apartheid in South Africa, actively opposed the death penalty, and in 1983, she fought to amend America's Civil Rights Act to include LGBTQ+ people.

Up until her death at 78, Coretta never stopped calling for peace and nonviolence.

> 66
> *Struggle is a never-ending process. Freedom is never really won; you earn it and win it in every generation.*
> 99

I HAVE A DREAM

One of the most influential leaders in US history, Martin Luther King, Jr. was a civil rights activist who devoted his life to advancing racial equality.

Martin Luther King, Jr. was a dreamer who turned his vision into action. Long before he became famous for his epic speeches, he envisaged a world where his children and all people "... *will one day live in a nation where they will not be judged by the color of their skin but the content of their character.*"

The son of a preacher, Martin, who was born Michael, moved forward two grades at high school, which earned him admission to the prestigious Morehouse University at age 15. Inspired by his religious father, he later earned a doctorate in divinity.

In 1955, he became the spokesperson for the Montgomery Bus Boycott, a campaign to stop segregation on city buses. He increased support for civil rights by organizing peaceful protests.

Martin helped organize the March on Washington for Jobs and Freedom in 1963, and delivered his famous "I Have a Dream" speech. A year later, the United States Congress passed the Civil Rights Act outlawing segregation.

In 1964, Martin won the Nobel Peace Prize and helped pass the Voting Rights Act. Although he didn't get to live to see his dream of racial and economic equality for all people realized, the man who said, "*only in the darkness can you see the stars*" created a brighter future for generations to come.

Today, Martin Luther King Day is a federal holiday in the US. It is observed on the third Monday of January each year.

MARIAMA BÂ (1929-1981)

Mariama Bâ was a Senegalese author and women's rights activist whose books were translated into over a dozen languages.

Born in Dakar, Senegal, Mariama was raised by her grandparents in a Muslim household. As an adult she worked as a teacher before her interests in politics and the injustices she saw pushed her to write. *So Long a Letter*, her prize-winning debut novel, explores women's lives and struggles in West Africa. Her later works explored similar themes, and Mariama used her voice to advocate for social change, including better education for girls.

One of the first Black African women to become globally recognized in literature, Mariama earned the Noma Award for Publishing in 1980.

Mariama is honored in Senegal today, with one of the country's top schools for girls named after her.

GLADYS MAE WEST (1930-PRESENT)

Mathematician Gladys Mae West played an instrumental role in the invention of the Global Positioning System (GPS).

Gladys was born in Sutherland, Virginia. Although she helped on the family farm, she knew early on that she wanted a different life. Education was her way out. Gladys worked hard and earned a scholarship to Virginia State College where she eventually earned a master's degree in mathematics. Gladys went on to work as a computer programmer for a naval base where she thrived for 42 years.

One achievement was her role in creating programs and collecting data that would later become GPS—a network of satellites that can be used to pinpoint the exact locations of things on Earth. A true STEM hero, Gladys was inducted into the Air Force Space and Missile Pioneers Hall of Fame in 2018.

CHINUA ACHEBE (1930-2013)

Chinua Achebe was an award-winning writer and critic. His masterwork *Things Fall Apart* has been translated into over 50 languages and sold 10 million copies since its publication in 1958.

Albert Chinualumogu Achebe, was born in the village of Ogidi on land then known as the Nigeria Protectorate, occupied by the British. At school, his teachers pushed students to follow Western traditions. However, it would be the Igbo folktales, songs, and proverbs he learned as a youth that inspired his future storytelling and expressive characters. As an adult, Chinua spoke out against colonialism, and his novels and writings explored African culture and the destructive impact of European occupation on African society. He remains one of Africa's best-known novelists, and he is commemorated each year at the Chinua Achebe Literary Festival in Awka, the capital city of Anambra State, Nigeria.

> If you don't like someone's story, write your own.

> I knew deep in my heart that nothing was getting in my way.

ALVIN AILEY

(1931–1989)

U.S.A.

Visionary dancer, director, and choreographer Alvin Ailey inspired and united people through movement. His dance company was admired throughout the world for its celebration of African American culture and modern dance.

Born in rural Texas during a time of economic depression and widespread racial violence in the southern US, Alvin Ailey Jr. was raised by his mother, Lula. Life was challenging, and Lula struggled to find work. The practice of racial segregation made things harder, too. But Alvin took comfort in the sanctuary of the church. His later work was steeped in memories of the rural, Black, church-going communities where he grew up.

In 1942, Alvin moved to Los Angeles with his family. Here, he snuck out in the evenings to local dance halls to watch people dance. When he saw his first professional ballet on a high school field trip, he was truly inspired and later began taking dance lessons.

After college, Alvin performed with the Lester Horton Dance Theater, rising up to become artistic director. Soon after, Alvin moved to New York City, taking acting courses and dancing with Martha Graham (a renowned American dancer) and others. A skillful performer, he dazzled in various Broadway shows, including as the lead dancer in *Jamaica* in 1957.

In 1958, Ailey founded his own company, the Alvin Ailey American Dance Theater, one of the first companies to welcome dancers of all backgrounds. His choreography celebrated Black culture and the Black community in America. "Revelations," Alvin's masterwork, remains one of the most performed modern dance works of the 20th century. Throughout his life, he promoted arts in education, founding a dance school and junior ensemble to help bring dance to all people. Alvin died aged 58, but in 2014 he was posthumously awarded the Presidential Medal of Freedom.

> 66
> *Dance is for everybody. I believe that the dance came from the people and that it should always be delivered back to the people.*
> 99

TONI MORRISON

(1931-2019)

LORAIN, OHIO · USA

Novelist Toni Morrison was the first African-American woman to receive the Nobel Prize in literature.

Toni was born to a working-class family in Ohio. Her parents inspired her interest in music, reading, and folklore.

She grew up in a mixed neighborhood, and said she didn't develop a full understanding of racism until her teen years. She said, *"When I was in first grade, nobody thought I was inferior. I was the only black in the class and the only child who could read."*

Studious and driven, Toni graduated with honors. She moved to Washington, D.C. to study at Howard University, and later Cornell University in New York. Later, Toni became a professor and published her first novel, *The Bluest Eye*.

Toni's dedication to her craft led to her winning the Pulitzer Prize, the Nobel Prize, and the Presidential Medal of Freedom.

MIRIAM MAKEBA

(1932-2008)

Singer, actor, and anti-apartheid activist Miriam Makeba (AKA Mama Afrika) was the first Grammy award-winning African vocalist.

Miriam was born to a Swazi mother and a Xhosa father and raised in a segregated township outside Johannesburg. Growing up, Miriam sang at church and school, and in her early twenties she joined several bands as a singer.

While touring and performing in South Africa, Miriam experienced and witnessed the terrible discrimination of the apartheid system.

In 1959, Miriam starred in an anti-apartheid film, which brought her international attention. Soon, she was performing in Europe and the United States. Angered by Miriam's criticism, the South African government exiled her. But Miriam had befriended many American performers, including successful Black singer-songwriter Harry Belafonte, who helped her settle

in the United States and encouraged her career. Miriam continued to speak out and call for change in South Africa and became involved in civil and human rights movements around the world. Her music flourished, too. Her fusion of jazz, folk, and traditional African music was a big hit with listeners.

In 1991, after more than 30 years, Miriam returned to perform in South Africa when apartheid was ending and anti-apartheid leader Nelson Mandela asked her to come home.

SOUTH AFRICA

" I kept my culture. I kept the music of my roots. "

NINA SIMONE

(1933–2003)

TRYON, NORTH CAROLINA USA

Known for her honest lyrics and fiery performances, singer, pianist, and civil rights activist Nina Simone broke cultural barriers.

At three, Nina began playing piano before she could reach the pedals. A lonely child, she took comfort in connecting with others through music.

Nina trained to become a classical pianist from age six onward. At 12, her recital was interrupted by the discord of discrimination. When Nina's parents were removed from their seats, she demanded their return to the front row.

Her community believed in her gifts and helped fundraise for her education at the Julliard School of Music. When her money ran out, she played jazz at clubs to support herself. She gained a following and, in 1957, her Top 20 track "I Loves You Porgy" introduced her to the world stage.

Nina also used her voice as a megaphone for the civil rights movement in the sixties. She said, *"There's no excuse for young people not knowing who the heroes and heroines were."* Enraged by racial injustice in the US, she lived abroad from 1973 until her death.

ANNIE EASLEY

(1933-2011)

> " As my mother said, you can be anything you want to be, but you have to work at it. "

U.S.A.

Computer scientist and mathematician Annie Easley broke down barriers in STEM. Her work helped Americans get to the Moon.

Annie was born and raised in Birmingham, Alabama. Despite segregation making it harder for Black students to access school resources,

Annie graduated at the top of her class as valedictorian. After majoring in pharmacy for a few years at college, she changed her focus to mathematics.

When Annie was hired by the National Advisory Committee for Aeronautics (later NASA) in 1955, she was one of just four Black computation staff out of 2,500 employees. For the next 34 years, she served as a vital member of

NASA's software development team. Though she had good times at work, Annie also experienced discrimination because of her skin color. She later became an equal employment opportunity counselor to help her workplace advance equality.

Annie showed other Black women that a career in STEM was achievable and her story still inspires today.

NGŨGĨ WA THIONG'O
(1938-PRESENT)

Award-winning Kenyan author, academic, and social activist Ngũgĩ wa Thiong'o, is one of East Africa's foremost literary figures.

James Thiong'o Ngũgĩ was born in Limuru, Kenya, when it was a British colony. He lived through the Mau Mau Uprising (a war for independence from the British)—a subject he explored in his first novel, *Weep Not, Child*. His painful experiences with colonialism led him to reclaim his traditional name and write in his Gikuyu Bantu language. Ngũgĩ's novels, plays, and essays often explore and critique Kenyan society and the inequalities and injustices within it. He has faced imprisonment, exile, and violence to silence him, but he continues to write and speak out.

KENYA

" Written words can also sing. "

FELA KUTI (1938-1997)

Singer and activist Fela Aníkúlápó-Kuti, AKA "Fela," was a pioneer of Afrobeat music, combining funk, jazz, and West African rhythms.

Fela was born to an affluent family in Nigeria when it was a British colony. Fela's mother, Funmilayo Ransome-Kuti, was a well-known women's rights activist, and his father was a minister. In the 1950s, Fela traveled to London and enrolled at Trinity College of Music. He excelled as a trumpeter, vocalist, saxophonist, guitarist, drummer, and pianist.

On his return to Nigeria, Fela formed his band and began to tour and gain fans. Nigerian authorities detained and beat him for speaking up against cruelty and greed, but he continued to use his performances to speak truth to power. When Fela died, 1 million people gathered for a funeral march to honor his memory.

NIGERIA

" The human spirit is stronger than any government or institution. "

KOFI ANNAN
KUMASI, GHANA
(1938-2018)

Knowledge is Power

Ghanaian diplomat Kofi Annan was the former Secretary-General of the United Nations and a recipient of the Nobel Peace Prize.

Kofi and his twin sister were born to an aristocratic family in Ghana, which was then known as the Gold Coast. He attended a Christian boarding school until his graduation in 1957, the year Ghana became the first British African colony to claim independence.

Fueled by his passion for education and his belief that *"knowledge is power, information is liberating,"* Kofi studied at four colleges in Ghana, Switzerland, and the United States.

In 1962, he became a staff member at the United Nations where he eventually became the UN Secretary-General and a special envoy to Syria. Kofi and the United Nations were jointly awarded the Nobel Peace Prize in 2001 *"for their work for a better organized and more peaceful world."*

JOHN LEWIS

(1940-2020)

Known as "the conscience of Congress," John Lewis was a civil rights activist and politician who served in the US House of Representatives for over 30 years.

Born in rural Alabama, John attended segregated schools throughout his youth. Teenage John became inspired by Martin Luther King, Jr. and met his hero at 17 years old after he was denied entry to Troy University because of his race. John eventually studied at Fisk University, earning a degree in religion and philosophy. During his student days, John joined and organized nonviolent civil rights protests, marches, and campaigns. He was one of the original Freedom Riders—a group who rode buses through Southern states in protest of segregated seating policies. John also co-led an important march for Black voter rights, which became known as "Bloody Sunday" after it ended in police violence against the peaceful marchers.

The courage he and his fellow activists showed captured worldwide attention and influenced the passage of the Voting Rights Act in 1965, meaning people could no longer be denied the right to vote due to race.

Later in life, John entered politics, where he used his position to help pass laws to make society fairer. Upon his death, the Presidential Medal of Freedom awardee was the first Black lawmaker to lie in state in the US Capitol's rotunda.

U.S.A.

" Get in good trouble, necessary trouble. "

EDMUND PETTUS BRIDGE

WANGARI MAATHAI

(1940–2011)

NYERI DISTRICT, KENYA

MAMA MITI

Wangari Maathai was a Kenyan environmental activist and Nobel Peace Prize laureate.

Wangari grew up on a farm in the Kenyan highlands. Her family lived among lush fruit trees and flowing rivers. She went to school when she was eight, even though it was rare for girls at the time. Early on, she became curious about how and why living things grow.

Later, she went to college in the US where she became inspired by the civil rights movement. When Wangari returned home, she was shocked to discover that many of her beloved trees had been cut down by builders. She found that the earth was dry due to the lack of shade, and crops were damaged. So she started the "Green Belt Movement" to plant new forests in Kenya.

Wangari led the charge to plant over 30 million trees and offer 30,000 women skills to build a better life. She said *"It's the little things citizens do. That's what will make the difference. My little thing is planting trees."*

Despite her death in 2011, the seeds she planted by standing up for nature continue to grow worldwide.

(1940-2022)

PELÉ
(EDSON ARANTES DO NASCIMENTO)
TRÊS CORAÇÕES, MINAS GERAIS · BRAZIL

Pelé is widely accepted as the greatest soccer player of all time, as a legendary member of three Brazilian World Cup-champion teams.

A shining star from the start, Edson was named after the inventor of the light bulb Thomas Edison. He was born to Dona Celeste and "Dondinho" Ramos before he rose from the slums of Sao Paulo to become the world's greatest soccer player.

When Edson wasn't in school or working in a tea shop, he practiced soccer with his father—a former striker who retired due to an injury. Since he couldn't afford a ball, he played with grapefruit and socks stuffed with paper and tied with string. Edson learned "ginga," from his father. Ginga is a style of footwork rooted in "capoeira," the movements enslaved Africans developed in the 16th century to escape captivity. Pelé's father inspired him to join a youth club coached by a former member of Brazil's national team.

Aged 15, Edson tried out for Santos, a professional team. He scored his first goal a year later, which sparked his rise to the national team, where he led Brazil's first World Cup victory at 17.

Edson's motto was *"Everything is practice."* The 1999 FIFA Co-Player of the Century said that dedication to the sport helped him achieve three World Cup titles.

CHAMP

G.O.A.T.

MUHAMMAD ★ ALI ★

(BORN CASSIUS MARCELLUS CLAY, JR.)

(1942–2016)

LOUISVILLE, KY • USA

Muhammad Ali was a world-renowned heavyweight champion boxer, famous for his unstoppable work ethic.

When Cassius was 12, someone stole his bicycle. He told Joe Martin, a police officer, he was going to beat up the person who took his bike. Mr. Martin told Cassius that he needed to learn how to fight correctly, and taught him how to box.

His ability to move faster than other fighters his size helped him win 100 out of 105 fights. In 1960, his powerful punches took him to Italy to win the Olympic gold. Cassius' victory in Rome led to a professional boxing career. As he prepared for a fight, he pledged to *"Float like a butterfly and sting like a bee."* His jibe turned into his badge of honor when he became the heavyweight champion of the world. Soon after, he converted to Islam and changed his name to Muhammad Ali.

In 1981, Muhammad hung up his boxing gloves. In the years that followed, the Presidential Medal of Freedom winner helped the United Nations provide food, medicine, clothing, and education to people in need.

ARETHA FRANKLIN

(1942-2018)

> **"**
> We all require and want respect, man or woman, black or white. It's our basic human right.
> **"**

U.S.A

Aretha Franklin was a singer, pianist, and songwriter. She is known as "The Queen of Soul."

Aretha Louise Franklin was born in Memphis, Tennessee but spent much of her childhood in Detroit and New York. Music was in her family. Her father, a Baptist minister, liked to sing and her mother was a gifted pianist and gospel singer. As a child, Aretha began singing in church and learned to play piano by ear. Life was sometimes hard for Aretha—her parents divorced, her mother died, and she faced many challenges, but she continued to make music.

At 18, she began to record for a broader audience, working with several record companies. In the late 1960s, she released her anthems "I Never Loved A Man" and "Respect," which catapulted her to widespread fame. Her incredible voice and mix of gospel and rhythm and blues captivated listeners. The civil rights movement was in full swing at the time and Aretha was applauded as an example of Black empowerment. She used her songs to call out for women's rights and civil rights and was asked to sing at the funeral of Martin Luther King, Jr.

Aretha had many achievements, including becoming the first woman inducted into the Rock & Roll Hall of Fame in 1987, winning 18 Grammy awards, and performing at President Obama's 2009 inauguration.

ANGELA DAVIS

Activist, author, educator, and philosopher Angela Davis is one of the world's most well-known human rights advocates.

Angela Yvonne Davis was born in Alabama. She attended a segregated school and experienced racial violence and injustice. The neighborhood she lived in was frequently targeted by the Ku Klux Klan, a hate group. These experiences had an impact on young Angela and stoked her passion for civil rights. As a Girl Scout, Angela and other troop members demonstrated against segregation. In her teens, she organized study sessions for students of all races, but they were disbanded by the police. Still, she carried on.

Angela studied at several universities and went on to become a professor, teaching students philosophy and feminist studies. She was an outspoken advocate of the US Communist Party, the Black Panther Party, the feminist and Anti-Vietnam movements, the LGBTQ+ community, and the movement to abolish prisons and the death penalty. In 1970, Angela was arrested. Prosecutors alleged she was involved in a crime committed by someone she knew. Her 18-month imprisonment sparked global outcry and radically influenced her future activism. She was found not guilty of all charges and released. The bestselling author continues to write, speak, and teach today.

66

You have to act as if it were possible to radically transform the world. And you have to do it all the time.

99

BOB MARLEY

(1945-1981)

Jamaican singer and songwriter Bob Marley is remembered as an icon and leading figure in reggae. His music and advocacy for peace and human rights spread around the world and made him an international star.

Born in the small, rural village of Nine Mile, Robert "Bob" Nesta Marley was the son of Cedella Booker and Norval Marley. His father left the family soon after Bob's birth and died when Bob was 10 years old. Bob was harassed for being the child of an older white father and a young Black mother and nicknamed "white boy" by his bullies. His painful experiences growing up would go on to influence his thinking and his music.

Bob spent his teenage years in Trench Town, in a government-supported tenement yard in Kingston. Although conditions were brutal and violent, it was also the birthplace of reggae music, with Bob as one of its pioneers. During this time, Bob explored different music genres (including ska), worked on his singing skills, and released songs. In 1963, he created The Wailers, a ska and reggae group with friends Peter Tosh and Bunny Wailer. The band, led by Marley's distinct voice, found success from the start and continued to grow and gain international fame.

A believer in anti-colonialism, anti-racism, and equal human rights, Bob used his music to share his ideas. When The Wailers split in 1974, Bob launched his solo career, with many of his songs promoting peace and love as well as highlighting oppression. His power was feared by some, and in 1976, he survived an assassination attempt. He continued to use his voice and, in 1978, Bob tried to help unite battling political groups in Jamaica by headlining the "One Love" concert.

After his death from cancer at age 36, Bob was honored with the Jamaican government's Order of Merit and laid to rest by thousands of mourners who visited while he laid in state in Jamaica's National Arena. Decades after his death, Bob's music continues to move listeners old and new, and his legacy of striving for peace and unity is not forgotten.

JAMAICA

"
Get up, stand up, stand up for your right. Get up, stand up, don't give up the fight.
"

OCTAVIA BUTLER (1947-2006)

Award-winning author Octavia Butler was a visionary writer of the science-fiction genre. Her books explored race, gender, women's rights, and climate change.

Octavia was born in Pasadena, California. A very shy girl, she lived with dyslexia, a learning difference that affects how our brains process language. Despite this, she found solace in reading and writing, and in the sci-fi genre most of all.

Octavia is best known for her books *Kindred*, *Fledgling*, *Patternmaster*, and *Parable of the Sower*. In addition to many awards given for her masterful writing, Octavia was also the first science-fiction writer to be awarded a MacArthur Genius Grant. Her fanbase continues to grow after her death, with new readers discovering her words.

" I began writing about power because I had so little. "

THOMAS SANKARA

(1949-1987)

Thomas Sankara was Burkina Faso's president for just four years, but his revolutionary politics established him as an iconic African leader.

Thomas was born in Yako, Upper Volta, a French colony at the time. He pursued a career in the military and soon rose up the ranks. His interest in progressive politics and his frustration with the poverty and corruption he saw led him to pursue a position of power, where he could bring about change.

After a coup, Thomas became president at age 33. He renamed the country Burkina Faso—"the land of upright people"—and quickly set about making positive changes for women's rights, healthcare, literacy, the environment, and much more. His time in power was cut short when he was assassinated, but his visionary work lives on.

BURKINA FASO

While revolutionaries as individuals can be murdered, you cannot kill ideas.

IMAN (1955-PRESENT)

World-famous supermodel, actor, entrepreneur, and philanthropist Iman is known for breaking barriers in fashion and business.

The daughter of a Somalian diplomat, Iman Abdulmajid was born into a middle-class Muslim family in present-day Somalia. After her family were forced to leave their homeland as refugees, Iman studied political science in college in Nairobi, Kenya. There, she was spotted by American photographer Peter Beard, who noticed her incredible beauty and spirit. With Beard's help, Iman moved to the United States and quickly became one of the world's most influential and sought-after fashion models. She was featured in magazines and became the muse of many designers, inspiring future diverse models. She branched out into TV and movies, started her own cosmetics line, and married rock star David Bowie. Today, she is also known for her charity work and for championing important causes, including education.

The day you settle for less is the day you will get less.

69

OPRAH WINFREY

(1954-PRESENT)

KOSCIUSKO, MISSISSIPPI · USA

Oprah Winfrey is one of the most well-known talk show hosts in the world. She is also a network owner, actress, and producer.

Oprah was born "Orpah" in Mississippi to a teenage single mother. Since her name was often mispronounced, she changed it to "Oprah." She was raised by her grandmother, who taught her to read before she was three.

At six, she went to live with her mother, a housemaid, who was away a lot due to her hectic schedule. Life at home was hard and Oprah ran away. Despite her difficult childhood, Oprah stood out as a talented speaker at school. Her gift for public speaking earned her a full scholarship to Tennessee State University.

Aged 19, Oprah became Nashville's first black female news anchor. Her success paved the way for her to host the world famous *Oprah Winfrey Show* for twenty-five seasons.

Oprah encouraged her audience to follow her example by "*Turning wounds into wisdom.*" Her positive message inspired millions, including President Obama. He awarded her the Presidential Medal of Freedom in 2013.

MAE JEMISON

(1956-PRESENT) DECATUR, ALABAMA · USA

Astronaut Dr. Mae C. Jemison was the first African-American woman to travel in space.

Mae set her sights on the stars early on. She was a curious child raised by a carpenter and a teacher in Alabama and Chicago. When she wasn't hard at work studying, she was dancing, acting in plays, and reading about science.

Mae was fascinated by astronomy and the workings of the human body. Her childhood interest in science and medicine led her to study biochemical engineering at Stanford University, and later to become a doctor for the Peace Corps in Sierra Leone and Liberia.

Mae said "*I always knew I'd go to space,*" and she pursued this lifelong dream when she returned to the US. She applied for NASA's astronaut training program and became the first African-American woman in their space program in 1987. In 1992, she soared to even higher heights as the first African-American woman to travel into space.

A masterful composer, producer, singer, songwriter, and multi-instrumentalist, Prince was one of the most exceptional musicians of his era and beyond.

Born in Minneapolis, Minnesota, Prince Rogers Nelson was the son of accomplished musicians. His mother Mattie was a jazz singer and his father John was a songwriter and pianist. He developed his passion for music early on and learned how to play the drums, piano, and guitar.

Music and dance were a source of joy and escape for Prince growing up. He mixed with other young musicians from Minneapolis, performed in bands, and worked as a guitarist. By age 18, he signed a contract with a major record label, Warner Records, and his career took off.

He released a new album every year, earning a name for himself amongst critics. In 1984, he released his sixth album, *Purple Rain* and made his acting debut in a dramatic rock musical of the same name. Both the movie and the album were huge successes. Prince soon became an international star and whenever he took the stage, he would wow the audience with his iconic style, genre-bending sound, stage-presence, and distinct voice. He became known for breaking boundaries and labels and was loved for his rebellious style. After becoming frustrated with his record label's control, he even changed his name to a symbol (see purple symbol on opposite page), becoming known as "The Artist Formerly Known as Prince" for several years.

Alongside his unique talent, Prince was also celebrated for his powerful partnerships and promotion of other artists in both music and movies, as well as for his activism, animal rights advocacy, and charitable work.

A Rock & Roll Hall of Fame inductee, Grammy Award winner, and Academy Award winner, Prince was named one of *Rolling Stone Magazine*'s "100 Greatest Artists of All Time." Selling over 100 million albums during his lifetime, and many more after his death in 2016, he remains one of the world's bestselling artists.

YANNICK NOAH

(1960–PRESENT)

SEDAN, FRANCE

Yannick Noah is a French tennis champion. He is best known for his 1983 French Open win.

The son of a French mother and Cameroonian father, Yannick followed in the sporting footsteps of his dad, a professional soccer player. During his childhood, Yannick devoted his time to training on the tennis court and even made his own tennis racket to practice with. His efforts paid off and caught the attention of tennis legend Arthur Ashe.

While training, he had to spend months away from his family, so Yannick turned to music to help with his loneliness. He said, *"When one sings, one does not speak about the problems of the every day. One speaks about the things which inspire us."*

By the age of 17, Yannick had won Wimbledon's junior category. He went on to achieve victories including the French Junior, Italian Open, and Benson and Hedges titles with his signature flamboyant style.

Today, Yannick's legacy continues through his charity for children, and his son, basketball player Joakim Noah. Now, he remains the only French athlete to successfully become a popstar after retirement.

JEAN-MICHEL BASQUIAT

(1960-1988) BROOKLYN, NEW YORK·USA

American painter Jean-Michel Basquiat was a street artist and expressive painter who collaborated with pop artist Andy Warhol.

The son of a Puerto Rican mother and a Haitian father, Jean-Michel Basquiat joined the Brooklyn Museum as a junior member at six years old. Fluent in French, English, and Spanish by age 11, Jean-Michel dreamed of becoming a cartoonist. After surviving a car accident, his mother gave him a copy of the medical book *Gray's Anatomy*.

He became fascinated with the structure of the human body and often referenced it in his art. He made poetry, music, and street art in high school, practicing learning by doing: "*I start a picture and I finish it.*"

After his graffiti tag became famous, he caught the attention of the art world. His paintings gained recognition throughout his twenties. Basquiat's imaginative mix of "high art" with pop culture—and his references to jazz, hip hop, and black history—catapulted him to celebrity. When he died, he left behind over 1,000 unseen paintings.

Barack Hussein Obama served as the 44th President of the United States of America. He was the nation's first African-American president.

Barack Obama was born to a Kenyan economist and an American anthropologist in Honolulu, Hawaii. He spent his childhood attending school and playing basketball in Hawaii and Indonesia. His experiences growing up in Catholic and Muslim schools expanded his worldview. He said, "*I benefited from a multiplicity of cultures that all fed me.*"

Barack studied at Occidental College, Columbia University. After graduation, he went on to work as a community organizer in Chicago before enrolling at Harvard Law School. After this, he worked as a civil rights lawyer and professor, penned *Dreams of My Father*, a personal story about race and identity, and served as a Senator in Illinois.

His commitment to public service and grassroots organizing secured his two election victories as president.

Michelle Obama is a lawyer who served as the 44th First Lady of the United States (FLOTUS). She pioneered as the first African-American FLOTUS.

Michelle LaVaughn Robinson was born and raised in Chicago's South Side. She lived in a tiny bungalow with her parents and her older brother. As a part of a supportive family who valued reading and education, both Michelle and her brother skipped a grade at school.

Her academic excellence brought her to Chicago's first magnet school for gifted kids, where she graduated as salutatorian. She went on to study at Princeton University and Harvard Law School. She said "*For me, education was power.*"

Michelle worked as a lawyer, city administrator, and a community outreach professional. As First Lady, she became known as a riveting public speaker, fashion icon, and advocate for military families, health, and wellness causes.

Barack and Michelle Obama have been married since 1992 and have two daughters named Malia and Sasha.

MALORIE BLACKMAN

(1962-PRESENT)

LONDON, ENGLAND UNITED KINGDOM

Renowned author of more than 70 books, including the Noughts and Crosses series, Malorie Blackman was the UK's Children's Laureate.

The daughter of Bajan parents, Malorie Blackman was born in London. A lover of literature, she read all of the children's books in her local library by age 11, including one of her favorite texts, C.S. Lewis' *The Silver Chair*.

Aged 28, Malorie published her first book, *Not So Stupid*, after working as a systems programmer. Before she found a publisher, her manuscript was rejected more than 80 times.

Her persistence drove her success as a prolific writer, and she became an Officer of the Order of the British Empire and the UK's first black Children's Laureate. During her tenure, she said, *"Reading is an exercise in empathy; an exercise in walking in someone else's shoes for a while."*

MAURICE ASHLEY

(1966–PRESENT)

ST. ANDREW, JAMAICA

Maurice Ashley made history as the first African-American chess grandmaster in the world. He is also an author, commentator, and puzzle inventor.

As a child, Maurice Ashley learned about chess from watching his brother and his friends play in and around the city of Kingston, Jamaica. Aged 12, he left his birthplace to move to New York City.

Throughout high school, he developed his skill and focus in Brooklyn's parks and chess clubs. Maurice continued to play in chess tournaments, winning game after game. He became the first African-American international grandmaster, which is the highest title that can be awarded in chess.

Today, the chess grandmaster and puzzle inventor is a commentator for the world's most well-known chess tournaments. He is also a coach to kids in Harlem, encouraging and promoting the game among young people there. Connecting his rise from the inner-city streets to the US Chess Hall of Fame, he declared, *"All those roses growing from concrete, just want a chance to live their passion and be great."*

OZWALD BOATENG
(1967–PRESENT)

Fashion designer, tailor, and entrepreneur Ozwald Boateng is famous for his signature style and artistry.

Ozwald was born in London to Ghanaian parents, who moved to England from Ghana in the 1950s. His mother was a seamstress, so Ozwald was introduced to clothes-making from an early age. He went on to study fashion design at Southgate College, and in his early twenties Ozwald used his mother's old sewing machine to create his first clothing collection, which he sold to a London menswear store.

Ozwald's star continued to rise. He dressed celebrities, became the first tailor to host a catwalk show at Paris Fashion Week, and the youngest tailor to open a shop on Savile Row (a street in London famous for its tailors). His iconic blend of classic tailoring and bold colors shook up the men's fashion industry.

For over 25 years Ozwald's hard work and creativity earned him many awards, honors, and opportunities, but Ozwald also gave back, championing investment in African businesses and ideas.

Today, Ozwald continues to design incredible clothes for runways, TV, movies, and more.

UNITED KINGDOM

" If I'm going to do something I'm going to do it well. "

BRIAN LARA

(1969-PRESENT)

SANTA CRUZ, TRINIDAD AND TOBAGO

World renowned cricketer and record-breaker Brian Lara is widely regarded as one of the greatest batsmen of all time.

The 10th of 11 children, Brian began playing cricket at the Harvard Coaching Clinic when he was six years old. His early education on correct batting technique helped him make Trinidad's under-16 team.

By the time Brian was 20, he became Trinidad and Tobago's youngest captain. Brian made headlines for breaking two cricket batting records in 1994, and for becoming the sport's most prolific scorer in 2005. He said, *"Like most sportsmen, I am very nervous before I go on to bat. If someone is not nervous, I am not sure what sport they are involved in."*

Today, the left-handed match-winner holds the record for the highest individual score in first-class cricket. Now a sports and tourism ambassador, Brian has traded his bat for a golf club. He participates in celebrity golf tournaments worldwide.

STEVE McQUEEN

(1969-PRESENT)

LONDON, ENGLAND UK

Steve McQueen is a British film director, visual artist, screenwriter, and producer.

In 1969, Steven was born in London to working-class parents from Trinidad and Grenada. Aged five, he showed artistic promise when Shepherd's Bush Library displayed a drawing he made of his family.

But Steve felt the impact of injustice early on. A gifted artist at age 13, he was disappointed that some students were given special privileges and others were pushed into manual labor roles. Sad about his school's lack of support, drawing became Steve's escape. He longed for creative black role models and struggled with his grades.

Steve's father wanted him to study a trade, but his artistic talent gained him admission into Chelsea College of Arts and later, to film school.

Steve went on to direct a film based on *12 Years A Slave*, a historic memoir about a free African-American who was kidnapped and sold into captivity. His movie earned him an Academy Award and raised awareness about the horrors of slavery. In 2014, he dedicated his prize to people impacted by slavery and declared, *"Everyone deserves not just to survive, but to live."*

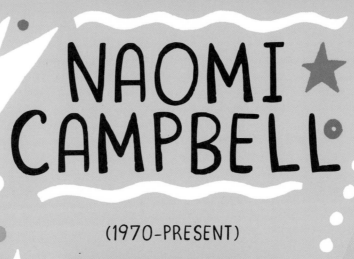

NAOMI ★ CAMPBELL

(1970-PRESENT)

STREATHAM, LONDON UNITED KINGDOM

Supermodel and actress Naomi Campbell was the first Black woman on the cover of French Vogue.

Naomi took the spotlight at an early age. She enrolled in stage school at three, and made her TV debut in the video for Bob Marley's reggae anthem "Is This Love" at age seven.

Naomi was raised by her mother, a professional dancer of Jamaican-Chinese descent. She traveled to Italy, where her mother worked, and lived with relatives while she was on tour.

Back in England, she studied ballet at the Italia Conti Academy. Aged 15, Naomi was spotted by the head of a modeling agency while shopping. She appeared on the cover of British *Elle* before her 16th birthday.

Naomi became the first Black woman to be featured on the covers of French and British *Vogue*, and *Time*. Her catwalk stride earned her spot as a supermodel for the world's top designers. Although she faced discrimination in a mostly-white industry, Naomi persisted. Saying, *"I will not shut up,"* Naomi speaks out against racism in fashion to help make the field more diverse.

MARCUS SAMUELSSON
(1971-PRESENT)

Marcus Samuelsson is an award-winning chef with restaurants around the world.

Born in Ethiopia, Marcus and his sister Fantaye were separated from their family during the Ethiopian Civil War in 1974. The siblings were adopted by a Swedish family and raised in Gothenberg, Sweden. There, Marcus was introduced to the art of cooking by his Swedish grandmother. His fascination with food led to culinary school, a move to the United States, rave reviews, awards, cook books, TV appearances, and one-of-a-kind opportunities, including cooking for President Obama's first state dinner. One of Marcus's most famous restaurants is Red Rooster in Harlem, New York. Marcus also invests time in helping underserved communities, and believes everyone has a right to good food.

SWEDEN

ETHIOPIA

66 Hard work IS its own reward. Integrity IS priceless. Art DOES feed the soul. 99

LIBERIA

66 I'm never afraid to speak truth to power. 99

LEYMAH GBOWEE
(1972-PRESENT)

Peace activist Leymah Gbowee is the second African woman to win the Nobel Peace Prize for her work leading the Women of Liberia Mass Action for Peace movement.

Leymah was born and raised in central Liberia. At just 17, her life changed when the First Liberian Civil War broke out. After a period in Ghana as a refugee, she returned to Liberia, where she trained in trauma counseling and worked with former child soldiers. Leymah knew women could be a force for change. She rallied women from different faiths to unite in nonviolent protests, which helped bring peace. Leymah's story has earned her many awards and inspired a documentary. She continues to champion peace and women's empowerment today.

AVA DUVERNAY

(1972–PRESENT)
LONG BEACH, CALIFORNIA USA

Ava DuVernay was the first black female film director to win a Golden Globe Award, and the first African American to win Best Director at the 2012 Sundance Film Festival.

As a child, Ava grew up near Compton, a mostly Black and Latino city in southern Los Angeles County. Throughout the school year, she attended an all-girls Catholic school, and discovered her love of movies while watching films with her Aunt Denise.

Ava often visited her father's childhood home in Hayneville, Alabama during summer vacations. Later, Ava said that trips to her father's hometown inspired her Oscar-nominated film *Selma*, about marches for voter equality in the 1960s.

As a publicist turned filmmaker, Ava attributes her success to creativity and determination. She advises aspiring directors to: *"Be passionate and move forward with gusto every single hour of every single day until you reach your goal."*

LAVERNE COX

(1972-PRESENT)

Famous for her award-winning acting and activism, trailblazing Laverne Cox was the first openly transgender woman of color to lead a TV series.

Laverne was born in Mobile, Alabama and raised with her identical twin by her mother and her grandmother. Growing up, Laverne knew she was a girl. She was bullied because of her gender identity, but despite pressures from some of her peers to conform to their ideas about who she should be, Laverne stayed true to herself.

She studied creative writing and classical ballet in college, before moving to New York City and focusing on acting. Laverne spent years working on her craft, acting in shows and on TV. In 2012, she was cast in her breakout role as a transgender prison inmate in the hit Netflix drama *Orange Is the New Black*. The role would launch Laverne into stardom.

Laverne proudly advocates for LGBTQ+ rights and has established a track record for breaking barriers and opening doors in the entertainment industry for future transgender stars.

> 66
>
> *We are not what other people say we are. We are who we know ourselves to be, and we are what we love. That's okay.*
>
> 99

CATHY FREEMAN

(1973-PRESENT)

SLADE POINT, MACKAY · AUSTRALIA

As the sixth fastest woman of all time, Cathy Freeman made headlines for being a champion sprinter.

When Cathy Freeman's family noticed her running talent, her mother urged her to develop her skill. A member of the Kuku Yalanji people, Cathy faced hardship due to economic instability and racial discrimination. In primary school, she was denied medals that were given to white girls even when she surpassed them on the field.

Despite roadblocks, she persisted: "You got to try and reach for the stars or try and achieve the unreachable." A scholarship positioned her to compete at Australia's National School Championships. This paved the way for wins in the Australian National Championships and the World Junior Games.

Cathy made history as the first Indigenous Australian to compete in the Olympics. Her trailblazing activity raised awareness about issues impacting indigenous people. When she won the Olympic gold medal in 2000, she ran her victory lap barefoot as a tribute to her heritage.

ZADIE SMITH

(1975–PRESENT)

LONDON, ENGLAND · UK

WHITE TEETH

Zadie Smith is a prize-winning novelist, essayist, and short story writer.

Born Sadie, Smith was raised by a Jamaican mother and an English father in London. A studious and creative kid, she spent her childhood developing her passion for tap dancing and musical theater.

Aged 14, Sadie changed her name to "Zadie." Inspired by her favorite writer, Vladimir Nabokov, she began shaping her literary voice.

Zadie went to study at the prestigious University of Cambridge. While there, the aspiring author worked as a jazz singer, and published short stories in a collection that caught the attention of a publisher. Zadie wrote her first novel, *White Teeth,* in her final year at university. The book, about three diverse families in modern-day London, was published to critical acclaim. It paved the way for her career as an award-winning author and writing professor.

When asked for writing advice, Zadie said: *"When still a child, make sure you read a lot of books. Spend more time doing this than anything else."*

CHIMAMANDA NGOZI ADICHIE

(1977-PRESENT) ENUGU, NIGERIA

Chimamanda Ngozi Adichie is a MacArthur "genius grant" award-winning author. Her writing has been translated into 30 languages.

Chimamanda grew up in Enugu, southeast Nigeria, as one of six children. Her father was a statistics professor and her mother was the University of Nigeria's first woman registrar. Chimamanda began reading when she was four, and started writing as soon as she could spell.

The majority of the books she read in her early life focused on British and American characters, who didn't reflect her reality in Nigeria. Although these books influenced her early writing, she says her discovery of African authors helped her "*Realize that people who looked like me could live in books.*" This inspired her to amplify her distinct cultural voice.

Famous for her lectures and writing about gender equality and the value of diverse storytelling, the author of *We Should All Be Feminists* and *Americanah* opens minds one story at a time.

SERENA WILLIAMS
(1981–PRESENT)
SAGINAW, MICHIGAN · USA

& VENUS WILLIAMS
(1980–PRESENT)
LYNWOOD, CALIFORNIA · USA

Serena Williams and her sister Venus Williams are considered two of the best women's tennis players in history.

The Williams Sisters are two of Richard Williams and Oracene Price's five daughters. While they are most famous for being two of the best athletes of all time, their bond as sisters surpasses their strength. Serena said, *"Family's first, and that's what matters most. We realize that our love goes deeper than the tennis game."*

Their father Richard, a former sharecropper from Louisiana, dreamed that his daughters would become tennis champions. He studied books and instructional videos to help teach them how to play by the time they were three. His coaching paid off. At four, Serena won her first tournament.

When the girls were kids, their family moved to a white stucco house in a tough community in Compton, California. Their father used their harsh surroundings to motivate them to study and work hard.

With his support, the girls sometimes practiced tennis on courts with dents and missing nets for two-hours or more each day. They trained so hard that they broke racket strings from hitting up to 500 balls with force. They developed powerful serves in the process.

Tennis became their refuge from the violence that riddled their community, and it elevated them to the world's stage when they rose to fame in the 1990s. Despite their unmatched talent, they faced criticism and exclusion due to racism and their unique style. They debuted within a year of each other as professional players, and have been making waves on and off the court as sportswomen and helpers for causes close to their hearts.

BEYONCÉ

HOUSTON, TEXAS USA

Beyoncé Knowles is a multi-platinum, Grammy Award-winning pop singer known for her dynamic vocals, iconic style, and dramatic video and live performances.

Although the Knowles sisters are both uniquely talented, they have their trendsetting glamour, dedication to social causes, and powerful storytelling in common.

Born to a salon owner and a businessman, Beyoncé was the first of two daughters. The talented Texan learned to dance, and won a competition with her performance of John Lennon's "Imagine" at St. Mary's Elementary School.

At eight, she joined Girl's Tyme, a five-girl act managed by her father. Although the group was defeated on a TV talent show, they persisted. This led to their transformation into Destiny's Child, which launched them into stardom.

The force behind the ensemble, Beyoncé rose to fame. Ever since her solo debut topped the charts in 2003, the woman who described herself as an *"Introverted kid who broke out of her shell on stage"* has remained an icon. All seven of her solo albums have hit number one.

SOLANGE

HOUSTON, TEXAS USA

Solange Knowles is a Grammy Award-winning songwriter, model, actress, social justice advocate, and soul-singing superstar.

Solange, Beyoncé's younger sister, refers to the women who visited her mother's hair salon as her "2000 aunties." She credits their influence with sparking her passion for storytelling and supporting women and girls.

The skilful songwriter won second place in a notable jingle-writing competition in elementary school. In her teens, she performed as a backup dancer for Destiny's Child and made her professional vocal debut on the group's 2001 holiday album.

Solange also built systems of support for other black girls in her mostly white private school, even starting a group called "The BF Club." She said: "*It was about creating a fellowship in a space that felt like it didn't belong to us.*" She never stopped her work supporting and celebrating Black women and Black culture. Today, she continues making music and inspiring others.

MISTY COPELAND

(1982-PRESENT)

KANSAS CITY, MO · USA

Misty Copeland was the first African-American ballerina to be appointed as a principal dancer for the American Ballet Theatre, one of the leading ballet companies in the United States.

Misty has always lived her life in fluid and constant motion. Frequent moves and conflict at home rocked her childhood, but she kept going.

After sleeping on the floors of motels with her five siblings, and regularly enduring hunger, Misty moved to California. Despite her harsh upbringing, participating in dance classes at her new school became a source of peace. She said, *"Finding ballet was like finding a missing piece of myself."*

While studying under ballet instructor Cindy Bradley, Misty found inspiration in the story and work of gymnast Nadia Comaneci and created routines to the music of singer Mariah Carey. Her endless drive led her to serve as the captain of her middle school's drill team. Later, it earned her a spot on the American Ballet Theatre's studio company and corps de ballet.

In 2015, Misty became the first African-American principal dancer in the company's history. Her spry agility in performances of *The Firebird* and *The Nutcracker* gained global attention due to her unique flair. This cemented her position as one of the few black performers at the highest levels of classical dance. *Time* magazine named her one of the "100 Most Influential People" for her pioneering work and her outspokenness about diversity in the dance world.

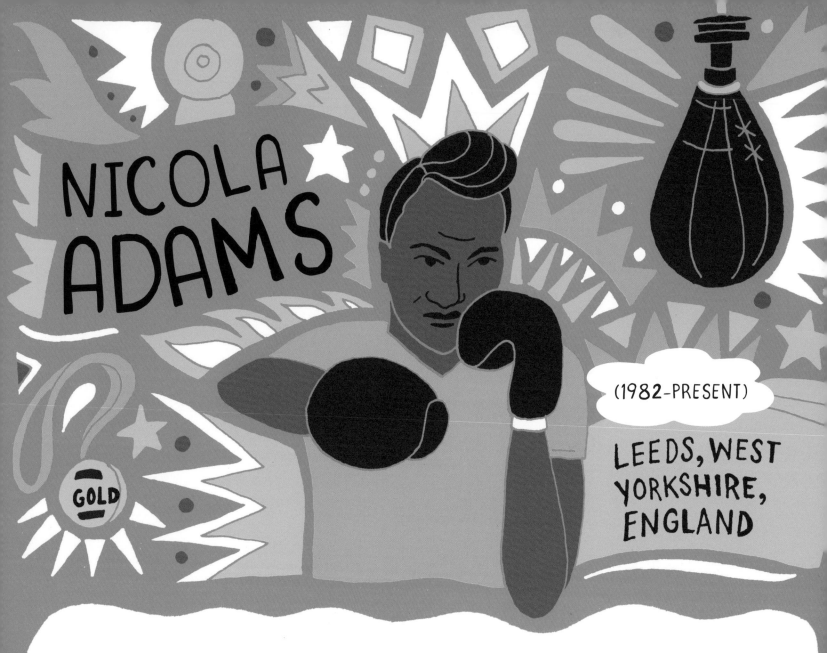

NICOLA ADAMS

(1982-PRESENT)

LEEDS, WEST YORKSHIRE, ENGLAND

GOLD

Nicola Adams is a professional boxer from Britain. She is the first woman to win an Olympic boxing title and holds multiple gold medals.

Nicola has been beating the odds since childhood. She grew up in a rough neighborhood in Leeds, where she found comfort watching videos of boxing greats like Muhammad Ali with her father. Nicola became inspired by Ali's graceful and quick moves and decided that she wanted to be a prize-fighter like him.

Despite being sick with asthma and allergies, she told her mother that she would win a gold medal for her fighting skills—years before women's boxing became an Olympic sport. At 12, she followed her mother to the gym because her babysitter didn't show up. There, she discovered a children's boxing class and became hooked on sparring.

Britain's most decorated fighter won her first match aged 13, despite a lack of opportunities for female boxers. She became the first female to win an Olympic boxing title after she won the 2012 Olympic gold medal in the women's flyweight division. She said, *"I just always wanted to win. I don't think about losing until it happens."*

MO FARAH

MOGADISHU, SOMALIA

(1983–PRESENT)

Mo Farah is one of England's greatest athletes. The long-distance runner was knighted after winning two gold medals at the 2016 Rio Olympics.

Mo's name at birth was Hussein Abdi Kahin. He was born in present-day Somalia, and he experienced a very difficult childhood. His father was killed when Mo was four years old, and aged about eight he was sent to live with relatives in Djibouti. He was then trafficked (which means illegally and forcibly moved) to the UK without his mother's knowledge. His trafficker renamed him Mohamed Farah and forced him to work as a servant. He began attending school at the age of 12, and things began to change. At school, soccer-fan Mo could show his exceptional athleticism and he also found a teacher to confide in about his home life. Soon, Mo was placed with a caring Somali family in the UK, and he could turn his full focus to what he loved—sports.

Although he dreamed of playing soccer for Arsenal as a child, Mo focused on track and field due to his stamina and speed. He developed his running skills in high school, where he began training with support from his physical education teacher.

Ever since he won the English schools cross-country championship at fifteen, Mo has been blazing trails and breaking records worldwide. The Olympian credits *"Honesty, fairness, and friendship"* as traits that help drive his success.

ESPERANZA SPALDING

(1984–PRESENT)

PORTLAND, OREGON · USA

Esperanza Spalding is a Grammy Award-winning jazz bassist and singer.

Esperanza Spalding was born to a mixed-race single mother in what she described as a "rough neighborhood" in Portland, Oregon. She was a curious child, and her passion for music from different cultures inspired her.

At age four, she discovered cellist Yo-Yo Ma while watching an episode of *Mister Rogers' Neighborhood*. Inspired by Ma, she taught herself to play the violin aged five, and performed with the Chamber Music Society of Oregon until she was 15.

Esperanza attended the Northwest Academy on a scholarship and studied the oboe and clarinet. In high school, she shifted her attention to the upright bass and started songwriting for a local rock band.

While at the Berklee School of Music, she began making waves with her unique ability to write music, sing in three languages, and play bass. She credits her exceptional style to her diverse influences, *"If you're a writer, and you write fiction, that's not all you read."*

Her openness to diverse influences sculpted her sound and helped her win the Best New Artist Grammy Award in 2011. As of 2023, she has won five Grammy Awards.

PHOEBE ROBINSON

(1984-PRESENT)

Multitalented comedian, podcaster, producer, actor, and best-selling author Phoebe Robinson is known for her relatable humor and powerful storytelling that amplifies and celebrates diverse voices.

Phoebe grew up in the suburbs of Cleveland, Ohio. She attended a private Catholic high school where she was the only Black girl in her graduating class. She dreamed of writing movies and, after high school, she moved to New York City, majoring in screenwriting at Pratt Institute. Following college, Phoebe wrote for TV shows, blogged, and podcasted. She started to perform stand-up comedy, talking to audiences about things she cared about and found funny. Phoebe then met fellow Black comic and actor Jessica Williams, and in 2016, they developed 2 Dope Queens, a popular podcast (later turned into a TV series) that centered around their friendship and gave a platform to other comedians of color.

Phoebe's meteoric rise didn't end there. She has created more solo podcasts, starred in movies, written books, launched her own production company, and continues to make people laugh with her comedy.

LEWIS HAMILTON

(1985-PRESENT)

Prizewinning Formula One (F1) racing driver and seven-time World Champion Lewis Hamilton is the first Black driver to win the F1 World Drivers' Championship.

Born in Stevenage, England into a multiracial Roman Catholic family with a white British mother and a Black father of Grenadian origins, Lewis Carl Davidson Hamilton was named after Black American Olympic track and fielder Carl Lewis.

In 1991, Lewis's father gifted him a remote-control car, which sparked his interest in racing. He started out racing karts at age eight. A hard worker with natural talent, Lewis soon reached the top of go-kart racing and by the time he was 10, he had won Britain's cadet karting competition. But Lewis wasn't close to finished. He had a big goal in his sights—becoming an F1 driver.

At 13, Lewis signed with the McLaren and Mercedes-Benz Young Driver Support Program, taking his racing to the next level. Two years later, he was the youngest racer in history to earn the kart racing's number-one position. Then, in 2007, he made his hard-earned debut as an F1 driver for McLaren and became the first driver with Black ancestry to compete in the series. His career has been at full speed ever since, with Lewis winning races, breaking records, and gaining fans worldwide.

In addition to his seven World Drivers' Championship wins, over the years Lewis has gone on to claim the most F1 wins, podium finishes, and pole positions—making him the most successful British F1 driver in history.

Lewis also makes moves off the track. He has spoken out against racism and the lack of diversity in motorsports, often using his platform to call out injustice. His charity, Mission 44 (named after his racing number), seeks to help young people from underrepresented backgrounds.

UNITED KINGDOM

USAIN BOLT

SHERWOOD CONTENT, JAMAICA

(1986-PRESENT)

Usain Bolt is a world-record breaking sprinter and the fastest human alive.

Before eight-time Olympic champion Usain St Leo Bolt became known as the "lightning bolt," he was born to grocery store owners in the small town of Sherwood Content, Jamaica. When Usain and his siblings weren't helping at the store, they followed their athletic parents' footsteps by running, playing cricket, and playing soccer.

When Bolt began to outpace his mother and father aged 10, they supported him by growing yams to fortify his body. Powered by a yam-fueled Jamaican diet and a zest for sports, Bolt began outrunning his classmates.

By the time he was 12, he had competed in the annual national primary school's meet for the Trelawney parish, and won the title as his school's fastest 100-meter sprinter. He rose to international prominence when his 200-meter victory made him the youngest World-Junior gold medalist.

Despite his speed and natural talent, Bolt struggled with repeated injuries related to a curve in his spine during his youth. As he grew older, he learned how to beat scoliosis as fiercely as he does his competitors—by keeping his back and core strong.

Although Bolt respects great athletes who paved the way, he proudly claims his current position as the fastest man alive, saying *"A lot of legends have come before me, but this is my time."*

UNITED KINGDOM

"
Write the tale that scares you, that makes you feel uncertain, that isn't comfortable. I dare you.
"

MICHAELA COEL

(1987-PRESENT)

Michaela Coel made history as the first Black woman to win an Emmy award for outstanding writing for a limited series.

Michaela Ewuraba Boakye-Collinson was born in London to Ghanaian parents. She grew up with her mother and sister on a council estate. The family experienced poverty, but Michaela loved many aspects of her childhood. In her late teens, she began performing poetry at open mic nights. She enrolled at the Guildhall School of Music and Drama in London, where she wrote the play *Chewing Gum Dreams*, inspired by her experiences growing up. The play's success led to the award-winning TV series *Chewing Gum*, which Michaela wrote and starred in. Her next series, *I May Destroy You*, brought her international fame and led to her history-making Emmy award.

Michaela continues to write, act, and direct. Her work often tells stories of "misfits" and people who feel on the outside of society.

U.S.A.

"To me, this is bigger than football and it would be selfish on my part to look the other way."

7

COLIN KAEPERNICK

(1987-PRESENT)

Colin "Kap" Kaepernick is an American football quarterback and social justice activist.

Colin was born in Milwaukee, Wisconsin and adopted and raised by Rick and Teresa Kaepernick. The Kaepernick family moved to California when Colin was four years old.

Growing up, Colin was very athletic. At high school, he excelled in many sports including football, basketball, and baseball. But Colin's passion was football, and he earned a football scholarship at the University of Nevada. His talent shone and in 2011 after graduating college, he was selected by the San Francisco 49ers. He flourished on the team for several seasons.

In 2016, Colin made history when he decided to protest police brutality and racism by kneeling during the US national anthem prior to each game of the season. Colin faced criticism and threats to his career, but many people were inspired and joined in, kneeling in solidarity. Today, Colin continues to champion causes that help fight inequalities in society.

KADEENA COX

(1991–PRESENT)

> "You just have to have heart, passion, determination and self-belief."

Famed four-time Paralympic gold medalist Kadeena Cox is the first British Black athlete to win a gold medal in either Olympic or Paralympic cycling.

Kadeena Cox is the daughter of Jamaican parents, Asmond and Jasmin. She grew up with 11 siblings in Leeds in the United Kingdom. As a child, Kadeena was active and brave. She cycled from a young age and was drawn to sports and dance. Her competitive sprinting career kicked off at age 15 when her field hockey coach saw her talent and encouraged her to run. Over the next five years, Kadeena trained and competed, winning races and earning a name for herself. Between training and competing, Kadeena also enrolled at Manchester Metropolitan University, where she studied physiotherapy.

Kadeena's life took a new path in 2014 after she had a stroke, which led to her being diagnosed with multiple sclerosis, a disease which affects the nervous system. Kadeena moved forward and developed new ambitions.

In 2015, Kadeena launched her Paralympic career and, in 2016, at the Paralympics in Rio de Janeiro, Brazil, Kadeena made history as the first British Paralympian in 32 years to win gold medals in two sports (athletics and cycling) at a single edition of the Paralympic Games.

Kadeena's razor-sharp dedication to her goals has led her to success after success. She has set world records in both sports, won medals, and inspired fans around the world. In 2017, she was awarded an MBE (Member of the Order of the British Empire), and in 2022, an OBE (Order of the British Empire) after winning two more gold medals at the 2020 Tokyo Olympics in Japan.

Alongside her sporting achievements, Kadeena has used her platform to speak out on issues close to her heart, such as body image and racism. In 2021, she founded KC Academy, an organization that is working to increase diversity in elite cycling by providing funding, support, and mentorship to diverse athletes.

AISHA DEE (1993-PRESENT)

Actor Aisha Dee was born on the Australian Gold Coast to an African American father and a white Australian mother.

As a little girl, Aisha grew up in a mainly white, conservative area. She loved watching *Sesame Street* and Hollywood movies from the 1970s. The diversity of the actors she saw onscreen encouraged her own dreams of acting.

At 16, Aisha moved to California, finding success as a teen actor on the Australian-Canadian series, *The Saddle Club*. Her star continued to rise and, in 2016, she was cast as Kat Edison on *The Bold Type*, a comedy-drama series that earned her rave reviews and many more fans. She is passionate about encouraging diversity both onscreen and behind the scenes in the TV and movie industries.

> " I'm hopeful we will have the opportunity to tell more authentic stories by hiring, promoting, and listening to diverse voices. "

ADENIKE OLADOSU
(1994-PRESENT)

Adenike Oladosu is an award-winning climate activist and ecofeminist who launched the Fridays for Future Nigeria climate strike.

Adenike was born in Abuja, Nigeria. After high school, she studied agricultural economics in college. She joined the environmental justice movement, calling for change and action to protect the planet. Her interest in ecofeminism was sparked after terrorist group, Boko Haram, abducted schoolgirls in Nigeria. She believed there was a link between this kidnapping and the drying out of Lake Chad, which devastated the area and led to more poverty and crime.

Adenike has spoken at global conferences about how climate injustice increases the displacement and harming of people across Africa. She has launched a movement to restore Lake Chad and is passionate about inspiring younger generations.

> " Becoming an activist is more than a choice for me, it's a necessity. "

NAOMI OSAKA

(1997–PRESENT)

Professional tennis powerhouse Naomi Osaka's groundbreaking 2018 US Open win made her Japan's first Grand Slam Singles competition winner.

Naomi was born in Osaka, Japan to a Haitian father and a Japanese mother. When she was three, her family moved to Long Island, New York, where her father began training both Naomi and her sister Mari to play tennis. The girls were homeschooled at night so they could train during the day. In 2013, Naomi went pro, representing Japan, and soon skyrocketed through the tennis ranks. A year after her 2018 win, her fierce and skillful performance saw her win the Australian Open, and become the first Asian player to be ranked number 1 in the world in singles tennis.

Known for her will to speak up about injustices, in 2020 at the US Open, Naomi donned seven face masks, one for each of her tennis matches, with the names of African Americans killed by racial violence. Beyond tennis, Naomi has branched out into fashion, skin care, and other businesses, inspiring others with her hard work and success.

JAPAN

" You just gotta keep going and fighting for everything, and one day you'll get to where you want. "

109

SIMONE BILES ★

(1997-PRESENT)

COLUMBUS, OHIO·USA

Earning more Olympic and World Championship medals than any other American gymnast, Simone Biles led the US Olympic women's gymnastics team to victory in 2016.

Simone Biles was flying high long before she defied gravity as the most decorated female gymnast in America. From competing with her brothers on the trampoline, to climbing a four-foot-high mailbox and teaching herself how to do back tucks, her adventurous spirit defined her early on.

Raised in Texas, Simone and her siblings were placed in foster care because their birth mother was unable to care for them. Her grandparents adopted her and her younger sister, providing them with a safe and supportive home.

After six-year-old Simone's natural talent caught the attention of a local gym coach, she began training. She developed her strength, practiced with her sister, and observed Olympian regimens to sharpen her skills.

Although Simone's drive helped her turn challenges into Olympic gold, her demanding schedule forced her to miss high school football games and dances. Despite this, her unmatched tumbling, flipping, and floor exercise skills paid off. She became the first woman gymnast since 1974 to win four consecutive all-around titles at the US National Gymnastics Championships, and the first female ever to be the all-around world champion three years in a row. Of her experience, she said: "*Making history is cool.*"

Simone, the shortest of all of the 555 American athletes at the 2016 Olympics, rises above the rest in life and sport. She made headlines for saying, "*smiling doesn't win gold medals*" when a *Dancing with the Stars* host criticized her for not smiling enough during her flawless routine.

AMANDA GORMAN

Poetic phenom, spoken word artist, and activist Amanda Gorman is the first person to be named National Youth Poet Laureate of the United States. She made history as the youngest inaugural poet in the nation's history when she recited her poem "The Hill We Climb" at President Joe Biden's 2021 inauguration.

Amanda was raised by her mother, a middle-school teacher, with her siblings, in the Watts neighborhood in Los Angeles. Amanda experienced challenges with speech and struggled to pronounce the letter "r" due to an auditory processing condition affecting how people register what they hear. Poetry became an accessible way for Amanda to express herself.

Despite the frustrations of having some people mistake her accent due to her speech impediment, Amanda found ways to work on her speech that brought her joy, including listening to songs she loved on repeat. She also gained inspiration to use her voice by wearing a necklace from her ancestor Amanda, a formerly enslaved person who could not read or write. Wearing her namesake's jewelry helped her soothe her nerves and gain confidence.

Inspired by Nobel Prize laureate Malala Yousafzai's global social change work, Amanda joined the United Nations Youth Delegate Programme in 2013 and later spoke at the UN Summit. By age 16, she had been selected to be the first Youth Poet Laureate of Los Angeles and published a poetry collection. Two years later, she founded One Pen One Page, an organization offering free creative writing programs for underprivileged youth.

Amanda gained worldwide recognition after sharing her words at President Joe Biden's inauguration in 2021. New readers and listeners around the globe were introduced to her poetry, which explores social justice issues such as race, feminism, and climate change. Just one month later, she accomplished another first—reciting the first-ever original poem at the Super Bowl.

Today, Amanda holds a degree in sociology from Harvard University and continues to make her mark as an author, poet, fashion model, and social justice advocate.

> 66
> *There is always light. If only we were brave enough to see it. If only we're brave enough to be it.*
> 99

NTANDO MAHLANGU
(2002-PRESENT)

Sprinter and long jumper Ntando Mahlangu is a record-breaking Paralympic athlete.

Ntando was born in Mpumalanga, South Africa, with fibular hemimelia, which stopped his legs from developing below the knee. Ntando used a wheelchair until he was 10 years old, when he was fitted for his first "running blade" prosthetics, thanks to a local charity called Jumping Kids. From then on, Ntando began to run and race.

By 14, Ntando won silver in the 200m at the Rio de Janeiro 2016 Paralympic Games. He has been breaking records ever since, winning two medals at the World Para Athletics Championships, and two gold medals at the Tokyo 2020 Paralympics. In the Netflix documentary *Rising Phoenix*, Ntando is seen racing a cheetah!

...I've learned to fly. I've learned to run and to be myself.

ZAILA AVANT-GARDE
(2007-PRESENT)

Lover of books, math, and basketball, Zaila Avant-garde became the first African American winner of the Scripps National Spelling Bee in 2021, aged just 14.

Born in Harvey, Louisiana, Zaila developed a passion for books from a young age. Her love of reading influenced her rise into competitive spelling. She also found inspiration from a Guinness book her parents gave her for her eighth birthday. The book of amazing achievements motivated her to earn three basketball juggling world records by age 12. Zaila's willingness to challenge herself and pursue multiple interests and dreams is an inspiration to many children around the world.

Multitalented Zaila has voiced two main goals for her future, so far: to work for NASA, and to play basketball for the WNBA.

MARI COPENY
(2007-PRESENT)

Activist and philanthropist Mari Copeny captured her country's attention at just eight years old when she saw a problem in her community and used her voice to speak up.

Born in Flint, Michigan, it would be Mari's hometown that first put her on the map. In 2014, Flint's local government changed the city's water source but failed to ensure the new water supply was safe. Residents noticed the drinking water seemed different. Testing showed high levels of lead in the water. Thousands of Flint residents were being exposed to dangerous drinking water.

Young Mari felt she had to act. In 2015, she sent President Barack Obama a letter about the crisis, introducing herself as "Little Miss Flint." Her words inspired him and raised awareness around the country. Obama traveled to Flint to see the problem and authorized $100 million in funding to help.

Since then, Mari has continued to call for change for her community and others. She has spoken at marches, raised funds for schoolchildren, and partnered with a company to produce a water filter so that people like the Flint residents can drink safely.

> " We need to protect dreamers, we need to protect kids in the most vulnerable areas, we need love and for people to care about their communities. "

TRAILBLAZERS

So many figures in *Shining Bright, Shining Black* forged ahead where there was no clear path, facing many harsh obstructions. In fact, many inventors, sportspeople, performers, and writers in *Shining Bright, Shining Black* "broke the color barrier," to become the first Black person in their place of education, work, or chosen sport, moving on to become leaders and inspirations in their field.

Here are a few highlights:

Juan Latino
First Afro-Spaniard to publish a book in Latin verse.

Albert Luthuli
First African awarded the Nobel Peace Prize.

George Washington Gibbs Jr.
First African American sailor to reach Antarctica.

Matthew Henson
First African American Arctic explorer.

Charles Drew
First African American to earn a Doctor of Medical Science degree.

Jackie Robinson
First African American to play modern Major League Baseball and be inducted into the Baseball Hall of Fame.

Madam C.J. Walker
First Black female millionaire.

W.E.B. DuBois
First Black student to graduate from his high school.

Thurgood Marshall
First African American to serve as a Supreme Court justice.

Shirley Chisholm
First African American congresswoman in America and first African American candidate to run for president.

Moses and Calvin McKissack
Established the first Black-owned architectural firm in the United States.

Bessie Coleman
First African American and Indigenous American to stage a public flight.

Nelson Mandela
First president of post-apartheid South Africa.

Toni Morrison
First African American woman to receive the Nobel Prize in Literature.

Mae Jemison
First African American woman to travel in space.

Oprah Winfrey
Nashville's first female Black news anchor.

Aretha Franklin
First woman inducted into the Rock & Roll Hall of Fame.

Octavia Butler
First science-fiction writer to be given the MacArthur Foundation "genius grant."

Barack Obama
America's first African American president.

Ozwald Boateng
First tailor to host a catwalk show at Paris Fashion Week.

Naomi Campbell
First Black woman on cover of French and British Vogue magazines.

Malorie Blackman
UK's first Black Children's Laureate.

Laverne Cox
First openly transgender woman of color to lead a TV series.

Cathy Freeman
First Indigenous Australian to compete in the Olympics.

Misty Copeland
First African American ballerina to be appointed as a principal dancer for the American Ballet Theatre.

Lewis Hamilton
First Black driver to win the F1 World Drivers' Championship.

Nicola Adams
First woman to win an Olympic boxing title.

Usain Bolt
Fastest human alive.

Naomi Osaka
First Asian player to be ranked number 1 in the world in singles tennis.

Simone Biles
First female gymnast ever to be the all-around world champion three years in a row.

Amanda Gorman
First person to be named National Youth Poet Laureate of the United States. She was 16 years old at the time.

POWERFUL PROFESSIONS

Each person in this book was included for the same reason: their power to inspire! But each figure was also an individual, with their own story, their own passions, different achievements, and different professions. Here are some of the many professions these inspirational heroes had.
Can you see yourself doing any of these jobs?

Academic
A teacher or scholar at a place of higher education, such as a university. See Ngũgĩ Wa Thiong'o, Zadie Smith, George Washington Carver.

Ambassador
Someone who represents or supports publicly a certain thing in order to promote it and improve other people's understanding of it. See Brian Lara, Muhammad Ali, Mari Copeny, Iman.

Architect
A person who is qualified to design buildings and other structures. See Moses and Calvin McKissack.

Artist
Someone who draws, paints, creates sculptures, or makes other types of art. See Jean-Michel Basquiat, Bertina Lopes.

Astronaut
Someone trained to travel in a spacecraft. See Mae Jemison.

Athlete
A professional athlete is someone who is very good at sports or a particular sport and who competes in organized events. See Jesse Owens, Jackie Robinson, Pelé, Muhammad Ali, Yannick Noah, Brian Lara, Cathy Freeman, Venus and Serena Williams, Misty Copeland, Nicola Adams, Mo Farah, Lewis Hamilton, Usain Bolt, Colin Kaepernick, Kadeena Cox, Naomi Osaka, Simone Biles, Ntando Mahlangu.

Author
A person who writes books and other literary works such as poems, essays, or short stories. See Juan Latino, Malorie Blackman, Hans Massaquoi, Maya Angelou, Toni Morrison, Langston Hughes, Frantz Fanon, Chinua Achebe, Mariama Bâ, Ngũgĩ Wa Thiong'o, Zadie Smith, Octavia Butler, Phoebe Robinson, Chimamanda Ngozi Adichie, Amanda Gorman.

Biochemical engineering
A type of scientific and technological study and process that looks at using cutting-edge technology with natural or biological materials to make different products. See George Washington Carver, Mae Jemison, Madam C. J. Walker.

Botanist
A person who studies plants. See George Washington Carver.

Chef
A trained, professional cook. See Marcus Samuelsson.

Choreographer
Someone who creates dances and sequences of steps to music, often for an audience or a dance company. See Josephine Baker, Alvin Ailey.

Comedian
A professional entertainer or performer who tells jokes and funny stories to an audience. See Phoebe Robinson.

Composer
Someone who writes music. See Sister Rosetta Tharpe, Louis Armstrong, Nina Simone, Stevie Wonder, Prince, Beyoncé, Solange, Esperanza Spalding.

Computer Programmer / Computer Scientist / Systems Programmer
Someone who designs computer programs (computer programmer) or designs and constructs computer hardware (computer scientist). See Gladys Mae West, Annie Easley, Malorie Blackman.

Economist
Someone who looks at how people, governments, or organizations gain or lose wealth, and the decisions that lead to different financial outcomes. See the Obamas (Barack Obama's father).

Editor
A person who is in charge of, makes changes, or corrects the text on works of literature, including newspapers, books, and documents. See Hans Massaquoi.

Entrepreneur
Someone who creates their own business and takes responsibility for its successes and losses. See Madam C.J. Walker, Marcus Samuelsson.

Explorer
A person who travels to distant, difficult-to-reach, or previously unvisited places to learn more about them. See Matthew Henson, George Washington Gibbs Jr.

Fashion designer
Someone who designs and crafts clothing, often for high-end fashion that is made to measure or unique. See Ann Lowe, Ozwald Boateng.

Film director / filmmaker
A person who creates or is in charge of making films. See Ava DuVernay, Steve McQueen.

Judge
A person in a court of law who decides how a law or judgement will be interpreted and applied. See Thurgood Marshall.

Lawyer
Someone who practices or studies law, which is based on the laws and legislation that a country or area follows. See the Obamas, Thurgood Marshall.

Paralympian
An athlete who competes or has competed in the Paralympic Games (an international multi-sports competition for people with disabilities that happens every four years). See Kadeena Cox, Ntando Mahlangu.

Philanthropist
Someone who donates and/or fundraises substantial time and money to causes they believe in. See Iman, Mari Copeny.

Philosopher
A person who has studied philosophy, which focuses on the meaning of life as well as historic and present ways of thinking and forms of belief. See John Lewis, Angela Davis.

Performer
Someone who entertains audiences and viewers by acting, singing, dancing, or telling jokes. See Louis Armstrong, Josephine Baker, Sister Rosetta Tharpe, Sidney Poitier, Alvin Ailey, Miriam Makeba, Nina Simone, Fela Kuti, Aretha Franklin, Bob Marley, Oprah Winfrey, Prince, Laverne Cox, Beyoncé, Solange, Esperanza Spalding, Phoebe Robinson, Michaela Coel, Aisha Dee.

Physiotherapist
A medical professional who uses exercises and massage to help improve or address medical conditions affecting the body's physical movement, strength, or ability. See Kadeena Cox.

Playwright
A person who writes plays, fictional works, often with dialogue, meant to be acted out in a theater. See Alexander Pushkin, Alexandre Dumas, Langston Hughes, Sidney Poitier, Ngũgĩ Wa Thiong'o, Michaela Coel.

Podcaster
A person who makes a podcast, an audio or video program, and puts it on the Internet. See Phoebe Robinson.

Producer
Someone who is in charge of the financial and/or managing sides of making movies, plays, or TV series, sometimes deciding if a work is going to be produced or created in the first place. See Oprah Winfrey, Michaela Coel, Phoebe Robinson.

Psychiatrist
A doctor who works in psychiatry, which studies and treats people with mental health conditions. See Frantz Fanon.

Publicist
A person who works to spread the word and give out information about a product, service, person, or organization. See Ava DuVernay.

Screenwriter
A person who writes for the screen, including films and TV. See Maya Angelou, Steve McQueen, Michaela Coel.

Sociologist
Someone who works in sociology, the study of the systems and behavior of people in a society, or on a large scale. See Amanda Gorman.

Supermodel
A highly paid and successful clothes, runway, and magazine model who has reached celebrity status. See Iman, Naomi Campbell.

Surgeon
A medical practitioner who is trained to remove, examine, or repair a part of the human body by performing surgery. See Charles Drew.

Translator
Someone who communicates information that is first either spoken or written in one language, and turns it into another, either verbally or through writing. See Alexandre Dumas, Alexander Pushkin, Chinua Achebe, Mariama Bâ, Chimamanda Ngozi Adichie.

QUESTIONS FOR DISCUSSION

Each figure celebrated in this book is a true inspiration. But now we turn it over to you. Thinking about their fascinating life histories and achievements, we've put together 10 questions to help you think of your own goals, beliefs, and achievements, both now and in the future!

1 Malorie Blackman's first book was rejected over 80 times, but that never stopped her. She continued to work to become a bestselling author. Have you ever tried something and had to change course or try again? How did you respond to that experience?

2 All the figures in this book felt a deep passion for something, whether it was fighting for freedom and equality, or doing the perfect pirouette. Enthusiasm and enjoyment—and belief—in something can lead to an exciting and inspiring future. Can you think of three things you enjoy doing? Now try to think about the three best things about each of them.

3 Business leaders are great forward thinkers and planners who work hard for their goals. Ozwald Boateng used his mother's sewing machine to make a menswear collection from his home. Do you have any long-term goals? Have you thought about how you might achieve these goals?

4 The activists in this book—from Coretta Scott King to Fela Kuti—saw a world that needed changing and looked for ways to make it happen. Are there any things happening in your community, or in other parts of the world, that you would like to see change? Can you think of ways you can help make this happen?

5 Before every great invention, there is first a lot of thinking and learning. Often, inventors play to their strengths, for instance George Washington Carver used his farming knowledge to invent all kinds of peanut products. Think about your own interests or hobbies. Can you think of anything that could be improved?

6   Laverne Cox knew who she was even when she was little, no matter what her bullies said. Prince refused to allow record producers to force him to make music he didn't want to make. Forge your own path and believe in yourself! What are some of the unique and wonderful things that make you who you are?

7   Shirley Chisholm and Jesse Owens are just two of the many figures in this book who experienced segregation and racism but refused to let it stop their dreams. Harriet Tubman, once enslaved, went on to put her own life on the line to help others find freedom. How do you feel reading about their commitment to fighting for freedom and equality for all?

8   Nelson Mandela, Barack and Michelle Obama, Queen Nanny, and Toussaint L'Ouverture all had to make important decisions that would affect other people's lives. These inspiring leaders worked hard to make their communities, and their countries, more just. If you could make your own laws or rules, what would they be?

9   When Kadeena Cox was diagnosed with multiple sclerosis she shifted her goals and trained to be a recordbreaking athlete in the Paralympics. It can help to remember that unexpected changes in our lives can lead to a whole new pathway. When things have been tough, what has gotten you through? How do you show up for and support people in your life who are experiencing challenges?

10   Bessie Coleman, Matthew Henson, and Rosa Parks all took a chance for something they believed in and felt passionately about, whether it was exploring the Arctic, protesting racism, or flying a plane. If you knew you couldn't fail, what would you try? Think about the obstacles that might stand in your way and how you might overcome them.

TIMELINE

Juan Latino writes epic Latin poem *Austrias Carmen*.
1576

Peace treaty signed between British colonial government and **Queen Nanny's** Maroons.
1740

Toussaint L'Ouverture becomes Governor-General with a new constitution for Saint-Domingue.
1801

Haiti becomes independent, one year after **L'Ouverture's** death in exile.
1804

Decembrist uprising in Russia
1825

Moses and Calvin McKissack establish the first Black-owned architectural firm in the United States.
1922

Langston Hughes writes poem "The Negro Speaks of Rivers."
1921

Russian Revolution
1917

World War I
1914-1918

Matthew Henson becomes the first person to reach the North Pole.
1909

Bessie Coleman performs the first public flight by an African American woman.

Crash of Wall Street – Great Depression
1929

Louis Armstrong becomes the first African American to host a national radio show.
Jesse Owens wins four gold medals at the Berlin Games in Nazi Germany.
1936

Josephine Baker begins to operate as a spy for the French Resistance in World War II.
1939

Miriam Makeba performs in an anti-apartheid musical film and is exiled from South Africa.
1959

Chinua Achebe writes *Things Fall Apart*, a fictional look at colonialism in Nigeria.
Alvin Ailey founds his own dance company.
1958

Ghana gains independence from British colonial rule.
1957

Rosa Parks refuses to give up her seat on the bus, beginning the Montgomery Bus Boycott.
1955

Albert Luthuli becomes the first African awarded the Nobel Peace Prize.
1960

Bertina Lopes is forced to return to Portugal for her political views against colonialism.
Katherine Johnson calculates the flight path for the first American mission in space.
1961

Bob Marley creates pivotal reggae band, The Wailers.
Martin Luther King, Jr. marches on Washington, D.C. and gives his "I Have a Dream" speech.
1963

Angela Davis is imprisoned for supposed conspiracy to murder for 18 months, then found not guilty and acquitted.
1970

Gladys Mae West helps create GEOSAT, which leads the way to develop GPS.
1970s

Annie Easley forms crucial computations for rockets in Apollo 11 moon landing.

Nina Simone releases "To Be Young, Gifted, and Black," in recognition of her friend Lorraine Hansberry's Broadway play of the same name.
1969

Maya Angelou writes international bestselling autobiography, *I Know Why the Caged Bird Sings*.

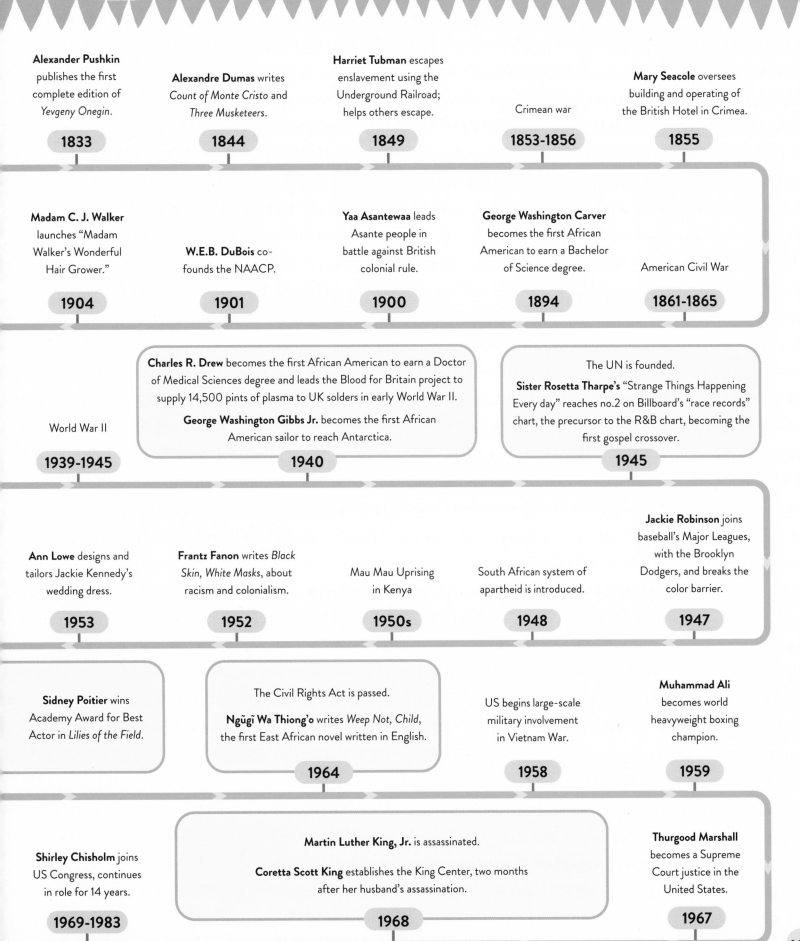

Alexander Pushkin publishes the first complete edition of *Yevgeny Onegin*.

1833

Alexandre Dumas writes *Count of Monte Cristo* and *Three Musketeers*.

1844

Harriet Tubman escapes enslavement using the Underground Railroad; helps others escape.

1849

Crimean war

1853-1856

Mary Seacole oversees building and operating of the British Hotel in Crimea.

1855

Madam C. J. Walker launches "Madam Walker's Wonderful Hair Grower."

1904

W.E.B. DuBois co-founds the NAACP.

1901

Yaa Asantewaa leads Asante people in battle against British colonial rule.

1900

George Washington Carver becomes the first African American to earn a Bachelor of Science degree.

1894

American Civil War

1861-1865

World War II

1939-1945

Charles R. Drew becomes the first African American to earn a Doctor of Medical Sciences degree and leads the Blood for Britain project to supply 14,500 pints of plasma to UK solders in early World War II.

George Washington Gibbs Jr. becomes the first African American sailor to reach Antarctica.

1940

The UN is founded.

Sister Rosetta Tharpe's "Strange Things Happening Every day" reaches no.2 on Billboard's "race records" chart, the precursor to the R&B chart, becoming the first gospel crossover.

1945

Ann Lowe designs and tailors Jackie Kennedy's wedding dress.

1953

Frantz Fanon writes *Black Skin, White Masks*, about racism and colonialism.

1952

Mau Mau Uprising in Kenya

1950s

South African system of apartheid is introduced.

1948

Jackie Robinson joins baseball's Major Leagues, with the Brooklyn Dodgers, and breaks the color barrier.

1947

Sidney Poitier wins Academy Award for Best Actor in *Lilies of the Field*.

The Civil Rights Act is passed.

Ngũgĩ Wa Thiong'o writes *Weep Not, Child*, the first East African novel written in English.

1964

US begins large-scale military involvement in Vietnam War.

1958

Muhammad Ali becomes world heavyweight boxing champion.

1959

Shirley Chisholm joins US Congress, continues in role for 14 years.

1969-1983

Martin Luther King, Jr. is assassinated.

Coretta Scott King establishes the King Center, two months after her husband's assassination.

1968

Thurgood Marshall becomes a Supreme Court justice in the United States.

1967

Oprah Winfrey becomes first female African American news anchor in the US.

1973

Wangari Maathai founds the community tree-planting Green Belt Movement in Kenya.

1976

Jean-Michel Basquiat begins painting graffiti with Al Diaz under the name SAMO.

Late 1970s

Fela Kuti records *Zombie*, an album criticizing the Nigerian military.

1977

Mariama Bâ's novel *So Long a Letter* wins the first Nova Award for Publishing in Africa.

1980

Ozwald Boateng opens a tailoring shop on London's exclusive Savile Row.

Octavia Butler receives the MacArthur "Genius" Fellowship Grant.

1995

Cathy Freeman becomes first Indigenous Australian to compete in the Olympics.

1992

Iman launches her own line of cosmetics for women of color.

End of South African system of apartheid.

1994

Pelé is awarded FIFA Co-Player of the Century

Hans Massaquoi writes a memoir on growing up Black in Nazi Germany.

1999

Zadie Smith writes bestselling first novel, *White Teeth*.

2000

Kofi Annan is awarded Nobel Peace Prize for his work with the UN.

2001

Venus Williams earns her first tennis singles No.1 ranking.

2002

Misty Copeland becomes principal dancer at the American Ballet Theatre's studio company.

Mari Copeny sends her pivotal letter to Barack Obama about Flint, Michigan's water crisis.

2015

Steve McQueen wins an Academy Award for Best Picture, for *12 Years a Slave*.

Laverne Cox becomes the first openly transgender person to be on the cover of Time magazine.

2014

Mo Farah wins two Olympic gold medals in Rio de Janeiro, Brazil, for long-distance running.

Lemonade becomes **Beyoncé's** sixth album to hit no.1.

Solange wins Grammy for her album *A Seat at the Table*.

Phoebe Robinson creates 2 Dope Queens podcast with Jessica Williams.

Usain Bolt wins his third consecutive Olympic gold medal for the 100-meter sprint in 9.81 seconds.

2016

Simone Biles becomes the youngest person to receive the Presidential Medal of Freedom.

2022

Adenike Oladosu founds grassroots movement ILeadClimate, advocating the restoration of Lake Chad in Africa.

Zaila Avant-Garde wins the Scripps National Spelling Bee aged 14.

2021

Aged 33, **Thomas Sankara** becomes leader of his country, which he renames Burkina Faso.

Yannick Noah wins the tennis French Open.

1983

John Lewis elected to US Congress.

Maurice Ashley becomes chess National Grandmaster (US). Thirteen years later he is chess International Grandmaster.

1986

Aretha Franklin becomes the first woman inducted into the Rock & Roll Hall of Fame.

1987

Mae Jemison travels into space.

1992

Brian Lara becomes Trinidad and Tobago's youngest captain of the national cricket team.

Nelson Mandela is released from prison after 27 years; four years later he negotiates the end of apartheid, and becomes President of South Africa.

1990

Toni Morrison wins Pulitzer Prize for Fiction for *Beloved*.

1988

Naomi Campbell models on covers of British and French *Vogue* magazines.

1987/1988

Prince is inducted into the Rock & Roll Hall of Fame.

2004

Chimamanda Ngozi Adichie's *Half of a Yellow Sun* wins the Women's Prize for Fiction.

Lewis Hamilton makes debut as Formula 1 driver with McLaren.

2007

Malorie Blackman is awarded an OBE in the UK for her services to literature.

2008

Barack Obama becomes 44th US President, **Michelle Obama** becomes the First Lady.

2009

Nicola Adams wins Olympic gold medal in the women's flyweight boxing division.

Ava DuVernay wins Best Director award at Sundance Film Festival. Two years later she wins a Golden Globe for *Selma*.

2012

Leymah Gbowee receives the Nobel Peace Prize.

Esperanza Spalding wins Best New Artist at the Grammys.

2011

Marcus Samuelsson serves up the first state dinner of the Obama administration.

Colin Kaepernick begins kneeling, in protest, during the US national anthem prior to each football game.

Kadeena Cox wins two gold medals (for athletics and cycling) at the Paralympics in Rio de Janeiro, Brazil.

Serena Williams wins her 23rd Grand Slam tennis singles title.

Aisha Dee stars in comedy TV series *The Bold Type*.

2017

Amanda Gorman performs her original poem "The Hill We Climb" at President Joe Biden's inauguration.

Michaela Coel wins Emmy for her TV drama *I May Destroy You*.

Ntando Mahlangu wins two gold medals (for long jump and 200-meter sprint) at the Tokyo Paralympics.

Naomi Osaka becomes Japan's first Grand Slam tennis singles winner.

2020

2018

GLOSSARY

Abolitionist movement An organized effort to end slavery. There have been abolitionist movements in countries around the world, including the UK and the US.

Activist Someone who campaigns for social change.

Advocate Someone who supports or champions a cause, idea, or action.

Allies The World War II alliance between the US, UK, and the Soviet Union (now Russia), along with smaller nations that fought the Axis, which consisted mainly of Germany, Japan, and Italy.

Apartheid A legal, political, and cultural system in South Africa from 1948 to the 1990s. It was designed to separate people according to their race and ethnicity.

Aristocrat Someone who belongs to the aristocracy, which is a group of people with inherited power over another, often larger group of people in society.

Autobiographical Based on the writer's own life or experiences.

Bigotry Having strong, unreasonable views and intolerance of differing views.

Bullying A repeated behavior such as teasing and name calling, intended to hurt someone.

Capoeira A combination of dance-like moves and martial arts, originating from enslaved Africans in Brazil.

Civil rights The rights every human has to be free and equal.

Climate change A longterm change in the planet's average weather and temperature patterns.

Colonialism The process of one country taking control of another country or area and its people in order to gain more power, land, and resources. A country or area under such control is called a colony.

Conform To be or act in agreement with something.

Cooperative action Collaboration, or group action, taken by people who work together to achieve the same goals.

Council estate A housing development in the UK built by a local authority and provided for people on lower incomes.

Coup A sudden overthrow of an existing government.

Discrimination Unfair treatment of people based on characteristics such as race, age, or gender.

Doctorate The highest academic degree from a university, after which the person can add "Dr." in front of their name.

Ecofeminism A type of feminism that explores connections between the oppression of women and ecological concerns such as climate change.

Equality Being equal in rights and opportunities.

Exile When someone is forced to leave or refused re-entry to their country.

Feminism The belief in social, economic, cultural, and political equality of people of all genders.

FIFA The Fédération Internationale De Football Association, the organization that governs the rules and play of international soccer.

Gender identity Someone's personal sense and experience of their own gender.

Graffiti Words or pictures that are painted, drawn, or spraypainted onto a public wall or surface, sometimes without permission.

Grassroots Used to describe a group, campaign, or movement that involves the people in a community from all levels of society, each with their own say.

Guerrilla tactics Actions performed in a sudden, unpredictable way, usually by small groups during a war or conflict.

Human rights Basic rights and freedoms that belong to every person in the world.

Indigenous People with long ties to a particular place. This term does not refer to a specific culture, but instead describes peoples and groups who have experienced dispossession of their original territories and assimilation because of the settlement of a more dominant group.

Ku Klux Klan The name of many different hate organizations and groups throughout the United States, which promote white supremacy and advocate violence, terrorism, and discrimination toward people who aren't white.

LGBTQ+ An acronym that stands for Lesbian, Gay, Bisexual, Transgender, Queer or Questioning, and plus, which represents other identities.

Lie in state A tradition where the body of someone who has died (usually an important person) is placed in a coffin in a public place so that people can view it and show their respect.

Maroon A person who escaped enslavement in the Americas and joined isolated communities that lived free.

Merchant boat A boat that carries goods such as food, spices, and clothing, to buy and sell, from one port to another.

Migration The movement of individuals from one place to another. People usually migrate to flee war, seek work, or rejoin family.

Muse Someone who is a source of inspiration for an artist, writer, designer, musician, or other creative person.

National Association for the Advancement of Colored People (NAACP) American civil rights organization formed in 1909, promoting social justice and advocating for the equal rights for Black people in the US.

Nazis Members of a far-right German political party that was in power between 1933 and 1945. Nazi policies were antisemitic (prejudiced and oppressive against Jewish people), racist, and deeply discriminatory and violent.

Nobel Prize An annual international prize awarded to people who have made outstanding contributions to the world. There are prizes for various fields including science, literature, economics, and the promotion of peace.

Noble Someone who belongs to the highest rank or class in a society.

Officer of the Order of the British Empire (OBE) One of the five Orders in the UK, created by King George V in 1917 to honor British citizens who have excelled in their field.

Oppression When a person or group in power controls another person or group through force, cruelty, or other unfair measures.

Outreach The attempt to bring services or information to people in their own communities or homes.

Phenom Someone who is extremely successful, talented, or admired.

Philanthropy Helping other people usually through donating money or other resources.

Plantation A large farm on which a particular crop, such as cotton, is grown.

Posthumous Happening or continuing after someone's death.

Poverty When someone does not have enough money and resources to afford and access basic needs such as food or shelter.

Prodigy A young person with outstanding talents, intelligence, or abilities for their age.

Protest The act of publicly expressing disagreement, disapproval, or rejection of something, whether it is a law, or a government, or an idea.

Racism Treating a person or group unjustly on the basis of their race. Racism occurs between individuals and operates within social and political systems.

Refugee Someone who has been forced to leave their country, often because of a war or another threatening event.

Sanctuary A safe place.

Science-fiction (sci-fi) Books or films about imaginary future events, often involving space travel and future technology.

Segregation Separating people into different groups based on skin color.

Sharecropper A farmer who uses someone else's land to grow crops, giving a portion of earnings and crops to the landlord.

Slavery When someone is treated as property by someone else and forced to work for them. An enslaver is someone who owns enslaved people.

Slave trade The business or practice of enslaving, transporting, selling, and buying human beings.

Social justice The belief that all humans deserve equal rights and opportunities.

Solace Something that brings comfort in a time of sadness or distress.

STEM Short for Science, Technology, Engineering, and Mathematics.

Township A residential area in South Africa, usually on the outskirts of towns and cities, reserved for people of color to live in during apartheid to keep them segregated from white people.

Transatlantic slave trade A segment of the global slave trade that occurred between 1500 and 1900. It involved Europeans enslaving and transporting many millions of Africans across the Atlantic Ocean, to forcibly work for white people in Europe, the Americas, and the Caribbean.

Transgender Someone whose gender identity is different to the sex they were assigned at birth.

Treason When someone tries to overthrow their country's government, often by working with their country's enemies.

Underprivileged A person or group who have fewer advantages and opportunities— such as education and wealth—than average.

Underrepresented A person or group who do not have enough people in positions of power to speak for them, help them, or inspire them.

Underserved A person or group who have limited access to or face barriers accessing goods and services.

United Nations International organization formed in 1945 with the aim to maintain international peace and security; headquartered in New York City.

Virtuoso Someone with outstanding talents or abilities, often to do with music or creative pursuits.

World War II Resistance An underground movement that involved individuals or groups working to resist or obstruct the forced occupation of their particular country.

To Pedro, always be your full self.—A.P.

To Mom and your infinite and everloving spirit. You remain my all-time favorite
"Well-Read Black Girl."
To Dad, my very first editor. Thanks for introducing me to Pushkin and beyond.
To Travis, thank you for the music and more.—J.W.

First published in 2024 by Wide Eyed Editions, an imprint of The Quarto Group.
100 Cummings Center, Suite 265D, Beverly, MA 01915, USA
T (978) 282-9590 F (978) 283-2742 **www.Quarto.com**

A CIP record for this book is available from the Library of Congress.

ISBN 978-0-7112-9716-6
eISBN 978-0-7112-9717-3

The illustrations were created in ink and colored digitally
Set in Futura, Buttacup Lettering and Azaelia

Commissioning Editor: Hannah Dove
Designer: Lyli Feng
Design Assistant: Izzy Bowman
Production Controller: Dawn Cameron
Art direction: Karissa Santos
Publisher: Debbie Foy

Manufactured in Guangdong, China TT052024

9 8 7 6 5 4 3 2 1